HANDHELD PIES

HANDHELD PIES

xxxxxxxxxx

DOZENS OF PINT-SIZE SWEETS & SAVORIES

xxxxxxxxxx

by Sarah Billingsley & Rachel Wharton / *photographs by* Ellen Silverman

CHRONICLE BOOKS
SAN FRANCISCO

Library of Congress Cataloging-in-Publication
Data available.

ISBN 978-1-4521-0214-6

Manufactured in China

MIX
Paper from
responsible sources
FSC® C104723

DESIGNED BY Design Army
FOOD AND PROP STYLING BY Paul Lowe
FOOD STYLING ASSISTANCE BY Mollie Rundberg
PROP STYLING ASSISTANCE BY Donald Purple
PHOTO ASSISTANCE BY Samantha Napolitano
and Kevin Norris

10 9 8 7 6 5 4 3

Chronicle Books LLC
680 Second Street
San Francisco, California 94107
www.chroniclebooks.com

Sarah's Dedication

For my mother, Karen Billingsley; my Grandma Nyla; and my Great-Grandma Bertha—three amazing women with a special skill for pie baking. I baked at their hips, and they passed along their tips, "the touch," and the conviction that lard makes the finest pie crust. And for Margot, my tiny daughter, who I hope has inherited the pie gene, to carry our family gift into the future.

Rachel's Dedication

For my mother, Linda; my father, Lane; and my sister, Rebekah—all of whom inspired me to follow my passion to write about food and supported me when I left a perfectly fine job to do so, but who must now patiently put up with my near-constant obsession about what we'll eat next and when.

CONTENTS

INTRODUCTION   8

Equipment, Ingredients, and Techniques   11

PROFILE: *Mamaw's Fried Pies*   22

chapter one
Free-Form Pies   25

Free-Form Pie Master Recipe   28

Chocolate-Cinnamon Pop Tarts   30

Peanut Butter and Jelly Pop Tarts   32

PROFILE: *Whiffies*   34

Orange Marmalade–Mascarpone Pop Tarts   37

Mozzarella, Tomato, and Prosciutto Pie   39

Chicken Chile Relleno Pie from Oh my! Pocket Pies, Houston, Texas   43

PROFILE: *Oh My! Pocket Pies*   46

chapter two
Structured Pies   49

Structured Pie Master Recipe   53

Pecan Pie   55

Buttermilk-Whiskey Pie   58

PROFILE: *The BitterSweet Bakery*   60

Pumpkin Pie   63

Farmer Cheese Pie from Four & Twenty Blackbirds, Brooklyn, New York   65

PROFILE: *Four & Twenty Blackbirds*   68

Bacon, Egg, and Cheese Breakfast Pie   70

chapter three
Jar Pies   73

Double-Crust Jar Pie Master Recipe   76

Banana Cream Pie   78

Coconut Cream Pie   80

Lemon Meringue Pie   83

Vanilla Malt Pie   86

Peanut Butter Pie   88

Chocolate Mousse Pie   91

Grasshopper Pie   92

Shepherd's Pie   95

Chicken Potpie   98

PROFILE: *Lasyone's Meat Pie
Restaurant*   100

chapter four
Nuts and Bolts   103

Two Pat-in-the-Pan Crusts:
Graham Cracker and
Chocolate Crumb   106

Flaky Butter Crust   108

Luscious Lard Crust   110

PROFILE: *The Original Fried Pie Shop* 112

Versatile Cornmeal Crust   114

Sturdy Cream Cheese Crust   117

Concord Grape Filling   119

Cherry Filling   120

Raspberry-Rhubarb Filling   120

PROFILE: *Grand Traverse Pie
Company*   122

Raspberry (or Other
Tart Berry) Filling   125

Blueberry Filling   126

Apricot or Peach Filling   127

Apple Filling   128

Dried Apple and Raisin Filling   129

PROFILE: *Hubig's Pies*   130

Pear-Ginger Filling   132

Sweet Potato Filling   133

Bittersweet Ganache Filling   134

Fresh Greens and Cheese Filling   137

SOURCES   139

INDEX   141

ACKNOWLEDGMENTS   144

Introduction

Thinking about why we wrote this book, and committing those intentions to the page, we both looked back over lives rich with pies. We could have told the story here of the rambling white farmhouse where Sarah's great-grandmother baked a dozen pies a day for her family, pies for breakfast, lunch, and dinner that fueled the work on a Pennsylvania dairy farm. Or of Rachel's quest for the perfect spicy beef patty, a flaky golden-crusted turnover carried to Jamaica by the British and from Jamaica to the Caribbean neighborhoods of Brooklyn, where she now lives.

But instead, we implore you: Bake pie.

We know that crust gets a bad rap. Bakers who end up with overbrowned edges and soggy bottoms routinely lament that making pastry is too difficult, too messy. Friends have confessed that they fear their rolling pin, that they nurture a special loathing of wiping up flour with a wet sponge, that their thick, clumsy fingers will never be able to handle dough. To these people, we respond softly, encouragingly: all you need is a wee bit of patience and a little time and you'll be rolling, folding, and fluting like a bake-off champion. You can do it! The folks at Grand Traverse Pie Company (page 122), now a Michigan empire, started with nothing: no farm, no family pie history, no pie-making lessons. In fact, they may have never even made a pie before they started down the pie-making path. Today, their cherry creations are ranked number-one statewide in a state that knows something about cherry pies.

There is little in this revved-up, complex, ultra-connected world that is more satisfying than pie. And we don't mean just eating it. We mean baking it, too. Making a pie can be as simple as a mix of butter and flour wrapped around a bit of sweetened fruit that gives up its juices, which thicken and caramelize in the heat of the oven. The rewards are bountiful and immediate. Your kitchen smells amazing. Your friends and family feel cared for. You earn the pride of a job well done. And, served warm, drizzled with a bit of cold cream and paired with a cup of steaming coffee, a slice of pie makes the world feel safe, warm, and complete.

Although we like pie in all forms, we believe our focus here, handheld pies, fulfills two more elemental pleasures: both small things and eating with your hands make you happy. Take them to a picnic or a bake sale. Stick them in your freezer and pull them out for lunch, a snack, or dessert. Carry a batch to a friend who has just had a baby and wait for her grateful call.

We want to teach you, or at least to inspire you, with tales of yumminess. In the spirit of encouragement, we have arranged this book for ultimate usability and convenience. The first three chapters are technique-driven, outlining a few different ways to bake small pies, with some specific recipes for our favorites. We provide you step-by-step instructions on how to make homemade pop tarts filled with chocolate (see page 30), how to bake a dozen little pumpkin pies in a muffin tin (see page 63), and how to build a miniature lemon meringue pie in a half-pint jar (see page 83).

The fourth chapter, Nuts and Bolts, is devoted to our favorite crusts and everyday fillings. These are perfect for mixing and matching; any of the crusts can be combined with any of the fillings to make a fabulous pie. But if you decide you want to master just one crust, go ahead and make it your staple, using it over and over with different fillings until you're ready for a change. You can also buy a top-notch ready-made pie crust (see Using Prepared Dough, page 19) and contribute a homemade filling. And, yes, you can still call it a homemade pie.

The pie universe is immense, creative, and delicious, so we had to think long and hard about what to include here. Sarah is obsessed with cream pies and can't quite decide if the coconut cream (page 80) or the banana cream (page 78) is her favorite in the book. But then again, fillings such as spicy-sweet apple (page 128) is forever classic, and apricot and peach (page 127) are two of the best ways to capture the taste of the summer sun in every bite. Rachel, who grew up in North Carolina, brought a sweet Southern charm to the mix through Buttermilk-Whiskey Pie (page 58) and Pecan Pie (page 55). She thought up the brilliant Peanut Butter and Jelly Pop Tarts (page 32), too.

We also had to make room for some of the great recipes from our friends the pie experts: the irresistible Chicken Chile Relleno Pie (page 43) with spicy gravy from Oh my! Pocket Pies in Houston, Texas, and the sophisticated Farmer Cheese Pie (page 65) from sisters Emily and Melissa Elsen of Four & Twenty Blackbirds in Brooklyn, New York, who learned their pie-making skills from their South Dakota grandmother. Redolent of thyme and honey, these little cheese packages may become your go-to appetizer.

Before we go any further, we want to explain how this book got written: We met in New York City and bonded over our curiosity about the world of food, whose magnetic pull we've both felt throughout our lives. Even though we live on different coasts now—Sarah in California, Rachel in New York—we share a love for small pies, and we knew our complementary talents made us natural partners for a book about them that strives not only to teach, but also to inspire. Sarah is the baker; Rachel is the journalist. Rachel researched and contacted some of the best small-pie makers in the United States and wrote the profiles of these fascinating folks that you'll find throughout this book. The recipes were all developed by Sarah, who also wrote their headnotes and all of the instructive text, in which she shares what she has learned over two decades of baking. Going forward, the *I* in the headnotes and text in the recipe chapters refers to Sarah.

This brings us to the ultimate truth about pies: they take time. All of the steps—preparing the dough, chilling it properly, making the filling, and shaping and baking your pies—add up to several hours. That said, you will spend these hours engaged in a sensual, delicious process with a rich, edible finish. A food processor produces excellent dough quickly, but you should give yourself time to make it by hand, working the firm butter into the silky flour with your warm fingers. The textures of the ingredients feel good. The movement is meditative. And there is no better way to develop a true feel for pie and to experience the satisfaction of handmade food.

So pick a pie and get baking! The sooner you do, the sooner you'll have pie in hand, pie in mouth. And in our experience, there's no better way to be.

EQUIPMENT, INGREDIENTS, AND TECHNIQUES

✕ ✕ ✕

Handheld pies are surprisingly easy to make.
But you will need some tools, ingredients, and
techniques to smooth the way.

EQUIPMENT

You need only the basics to turn out little pies: measuring cups and spoons, a rolling pin, a large bowl, a spatula, and a baking sheet (a few are even better). It is hard to make pies without these everyday tools (though, in a pinch—read *dorm room*—Sarah has rolled out dough with a wine bottle). Other pieces of equipment that simplify or prettify your pies are listed here, along with advice on choosing some of the basics.

Baking rack

When your pies come out of the oven, you'll want to transfer them to a wire baking rack so air can circulate around them, cooling them evenly.

Baking sheet

Free-form pies are typically baked on rimmed baking sheets. If you are making jar pies, the easiest way to transport them to the oven and bake them is on a rimmed baking sheet. You'll get them into the oven all at once, and they won't tilt on the bars of the rack. Sheet pans are also nice for catching the occasional leak from a bubbling filling, ensuring it doesn't run onto the oven floor and burn.

Cookie or biscuit cutters

These are handy for cutting out crust shapes. They can have a straight or scalloped edge and be circles, hearts, squares, or stars. Resist using shapes that have cutouts or narrow parts, such as trees, gingerbread people, or snowflakes. They are difficult to fill and some won't contain a filling.

Dough scraper

This handy tool consists of a straight-edged, broad metal blade attached to a wood, rolled metal, or hard plastic handle. It is used for cleaning sticky dough bits from work surfaces and for lifting, turning, and transferring dough.

Food processor

This proven time-saver makes short work of cutting butter into dry ingredients, of grating apples, and of puréeing fruits when a smooth, rather than chunky, filling is desired.

Frying pan or sauté pan

When frying small pies, you want at least 1½ in/ 4 cm of oil in the pan and enough space to fry three or four pies at the same time. A heavy, deep 10- or 12-in/25- or 30-cm frying pan or sauté pan with 4-in/10-cm sides works nicely.

Jars

The Jar Pies chapter explains how to make little pies in ½-pint/240-ml jars. You want jars that are wider at the mouth than at the base or are at least straight sided. It seems obvious, but this is a common mistake: you cannot pop your baked pies out of the jar if the mouth is smaller than the base. Old-fashioned canning jars are perfect and can be used over and over; just discard them if they are cracked, as they may break when filled or baked.

Muffin tin

Many of the structured pies in this book are baked in a standard muffin tin, with cups that measure 2½ to 3 in/6 to 7.5 cm in diameter. Tins made from sturdy, nonreflective metal work best. Sarah's are at least forty years old, quite dinged up, and perfectly great. Tins with twelve cups are easy to transfer in and out of the oven and rest nicely on the oven rack. Tins with six cups are easier to fit in the refrigerator. If you don't fill every cup in the tin, stagger your pies throughout the tin, leaving empty cups between pies, rather than loading all of the cups on half of the tin and leaving the other half empty. This ensures even baking.

Parchment or baking paper
Useful for rolling, wrapping, and baking dough, moisture-resistant, grease-resistant parchment paper also protects baking sheets from sticky pie-filling spills.

Pastry blender
This looks like a weapon but works like a charm. Essentially a short-handled masher with a series of rounded cutters, the pastry blender, also known as a pastry cutter, makes short work of cutting butter evenly into dry ingredients when making dough by hand. We both prefer a blade cutter to a wire cutter; blade cutters are sturdier and easier to clean.

Pastry wheel and pizza wheel
The pastry wheel consists of a fluted wheel attached to a handle. It cuts dough neatly and crimps the edges, creating a pretty finish. You'll also find that it is easier to roll a straight line than it is to cut one with a knife. A pizza wheel, which has a plain roller, works equally well for cutting straight edges. You should have both wheels in your tool kit. Or, look for a pastry wheel with a fluted wheel at one end of the handle and a plain wheel at the other.

Pie molds
Found at flea markets, antique stores, and in some kitchenware shops (Williams-Sonoma carries a good selection), pocket-sized pie molds do all the work of shaping a little pie: you use them to cut out the top and bottom crusts, to hold the crusts as you fill them, and to crimp the edges. Various shapes are available, such as apples or other fruit, hearts, circles, and bars. Some molds include a decorative cutout in the top crust that acts as a steam vent. Pie molds vary wildly in quality. Look for ones with a sturdy hinge, a minimum of nooks and crannies for dough to lodge, and sharp—not blunt—cutting edges.

Pie weights
When making pies in jars or in muffin tins and for pies with creamy unbaked fillings (such as Banana Cream Pie, page 78), you'll need to weight down the crust when you blind bake it (page 18). If you don't have pie weights, which are small, heavy ceramic or metal rounds that look like large beads, substitute dried beans.

Rolling pin
Heavy, wooden rolling pins are the best option for their weight and finesse. We find marble a bit too heavy, and also stickier. But you should use what you have or what you feel the most comfortable using. We have found that wood or marble rollers are more effective than plastic or silicone rollers—or a wine bottle!

INGREDIENTS

The general rule is simple: The better your ingredients, the more flavorful they are. The more flavorful your ingredients, the tastier your pies are. The tastier your pies, the happier you'll be!

Butter

All of the recipes in this book were tested with good-quality unsalted butter from an ordinary grocery store. Many excellent Irish, French, Danish, and other European butters are available in well-stocked supermarkets, and some farmers' markets and cheese shops carry locally made European-style butters. These naturally cultured butters are a treat to bake with and contribute beautiful flavor to your crusts. They are richer and softer than regular grocery-store butter, however, so if you use them in our recipes, you may need to scale down the amount by about 2 tbsp.

Flour

Our recipes call for all-purpose flour, but you can experiment with whole-grain flours and with pastry flour if you want to vary the texture and flavor of your crust (see Using Locally Milled Flours, facing page).

Fruit

Use fruit in season or high-quality frozen fruit. Of course, the finest frozen fruit will be fruit you freeze yourself. It's a good idea to buy a flat of peaches or berries at the peak of the season and bag the sliced fruit or whole berries in doubled resealable plastic bags or in airtight plastic containers. They keep well for several months in the freezer, carrying their bright flavors from the peak of summer well into winter's chill.

Short on freezer space or time? You'll find some good frozen-fruit brands in the Sources (page 139).

Lard

The rendered fat from a pig, lard contributes extraordinary flavor and tenderness to pie crusts. No, your crust won't taste bacon-y, but it will taste slightly richer and have a softer, more luxurious mouthfeel than a butter crust. And, should you fear the lard, know that it contains 45 percent monosaturated fat (the good stuff) and less saturated fat than butter.

Like all pork products, the best-quality lard comes from smaller farms and top-notch larger producers. Many supermarkets carry lard that has been hydrogenated to extend its shelf life, which you should pass up. Instead, you want to look for leaf lard, which is rendered from the fat around the pig's kidneys and is the highest grade. Sarah buys leaf lard with a gorgeous flavor at the Prather Ranch store in the San Francisco Ferry Building. It usually comes in a little pail and will keep in your refrigerator for several weeks or in the freezer for up to 3 months. Rachel buys leaf lard frozen in plastic pouches from Flying Pigs Farm at the New York City Greenmarket. (Flying Pigs also sells an excellent frozen butter-lard pie crust, which brings up the point that a blend of the two fats is also excellent, should you care to try it.) Prairie Pride Farm, located in Minnesota, sells a good organic leaf lard that can be ordered online from their Web site (see Sources, page 139).

Sugar

Many of the recipes in this book call for light or dark brown sugar. We believe it contributes a fuller, richer flavor. But if you like, you can substitute granulated sugar. You can also experiment with the richly flavored and textured natural sugars now available in most grocery stores, such as Demerara or muscovado. Because the crystals are often larger, these sugars are especially good for sprinkling, adding a bit of sparkle and crunch to your finished pies. You can use a colored sanding sugar, too, especially if you're making themed or holiday pies. Sarah's great-grandmother swore by superfine sugar, which dissolves more quickly in liquids and can be substituted for granulated sugar if you want to avoid a sugary crunch.

A Short Rant on Shortening

We do not use shortening. We know this is an affront to many of you—especially to Southerners who grew up loving the easy-to-handle dough it yields and its smooth taste in flaky baked crusts. But we simply don't think it tastes anywhere near as good as butter, lard, or cream cheese. Yes, it yields malleable dough and flaky crusts, but flaky yet flavorless is not what we enjoy.

Using Locally Milled Flours

A few seasons ago at San Francisco's Ferry Plaza Farmers Market, Sarah noticed a curious sight: a giant, hand-cranked mill set up next to one of the booths. She watched for several minutes as an older woman worked herself into a lather grinding enough flour to fill a modest-sized bag. Then Sarah stepped up to the machine and ground out her own bag (it took 15 minutes, the bag was equally small). Sarah took her precious freshly milled flour home and immediately began baking.

Nowadays, more and more home bakers can get their hands on locally milled flours. In some cases, these flours are made from regionally grown heritage grains on a small scale, which means they have a flavor that is distinct—sometimes nuttier, earthier, sweeter, downright grainier—from mass-produced flours. They are also typically free of additives and preservatives. The milling process is usually different, too. The flours are often stone-ground, which gives

them a unique texture that can be detected in baked goods. These flours are fun to experiment with and are often more nutritious.

Sarah experimented with several small-mill flours when testing the recipes for this book and discovered that there is no precise formula for using them. She found that she could not trade out 2 cups/255 g all-purpose flour for the same amount of small-mill flour. Instead, she had to play with the proportions to get a good result, and the amounts diverged in each case. Although we cannot provide hard-and-fast rules for using these cool small-mill flours, we encourage you, once you are brave, to experiment with them. Full Belly Farm, Butterworks Farm, and Daisy Flour are three good suppliers (see Sources, page 139). You will probably need to do some sleuthing to find small-scale milled flours in your area. Start your search by asking at local bakeries, farmers' markets, and food co-ops.

TECHNIQUES

We champion homemade pies. We are convinced that anyone can bake them. That said, a good pie is the product of centuries of pastry-making methodologies and wisdom, so here we've outlined some basic rules, tips, and techniques.

If you line up ten baking books and review the pastry techniques they contain, they'll all diverge and differ from one another on various points. The experience of cooking from a cookbook is learning one person's way of doing things. This section outlines what works for us. As your skill increases, you may develop your own tricks. You may consult other books. Go forth and do so, we say. Go with what works for you.

To start
Wipe down your work area and make space in your refrigerator to accommodate chilling dough and trays of pies. Rip or cut a few sheets of parchment paper. Measure out your ingredients, and make sure they're at the proper temperature (butter chilled, ice water prepared, egg cracked into a small bowl). Lay out your equipment, too. Rummaging around in drawers and cupboards with sticky, floury hands is a messy endeavor.

Measuring
The dry volume measurements in this book are based on scooping the dry ingredients into the measuring cup with a spoon, then leveling off the top with a flat edge. Using the measuring cup as a scoop or pouring directly from the bag into the measuring cup may result in different volumes of flour or sugar. In most cases, the brown sugar measurement is specified as "firmly packed." This means you press the sugar into the cup with your palm or a spoon, tamping it down as you add it in until it is level with the top of the cup. Measurements of fruits and nuts for fillings do not need to be this precise; if you have slightly more (because you want to use the whole basket of berries) or less (because you snacked on a handful of the pecans), just make a few less pies rather than stretch your filling.

Rolling
When rolling out dough, keep a small bowl or scoop of flour within easy reach for sprinkling on the dough, the work surface, your hands, and the rolling pin as necessary. Rolling can be a sticky business, especially if it's a warm day or your kitchen is hot. If this is the case, try to work quickly, use the dough straight from the refrigerator, and refrigerate the portion of dough you're not using at the moment. Also, make sure your equipment and work surface are cool and dry. When dough sticks to the rolling pin, wipe it off immediately with a dry, clean cloth or rub it off with your floury palm. And if you have a dough scraper, use it for cleaning the work surface and for moving the rolled-out dough around on the surface or to another surface.

You can also place the dough between sheets of parchment paper or plastic wrap for rolling (it is a good idea to sprinkle either one with flour, too). Know that getting the rolling started is the hardest part; after you've given the dough a few presses, the action can be meditative, or even fun. You'll develop a feel for dough at the perfect temperature for rolling. It will be neither too soft (and sticky) nor too hard (likely to crack and crumble). What you're looking for is dough at cool room temperature.

It has a bit of give to it when you press it with your fingertips, and when you make your first few passes with the rolling pin, it is pliable and yields evenly to the pressure.

Roll the dough in all directions. You can move the dough around or rotate it after every few strokes of the pin. Start by rolling three strokes away from your body. Then slide the dough scraper under the disk, give it a quarter-turn clockwise, and roll away from your body three more times. Lift, turn, and repeat again and again. The dough will be gradually flattening and widening more or less evenly on all sides.

Always roll in one direction, that is, not back and forth over the dough, but continually away from your body. You can start at the edge of the dough closest to you and roll edge to edge, but it is usually more effective to roll outward from the center (where the critical mass of dough is) to the edge.

You can also flip the dough over as you roll it out, to work it evenly from both sides. This helps to keep it from sticking. And if your dough develops wrinkles and rips, don't worry. Wrinkles or folds can be smoothed and will bake into the pie. Rips can be patched easily by pressing bits of leftover dough into them.

Shaping and Filling

For specifics on shaping and filling free-form pies, structured pies, and jar pies, see the master recipes on pages 28, 53, and 76, respectively.

Because free-form pies and fried pies are not supported in a jar or muffin tin in the oven, they must be well constructed. If the edges are not securely sealed, the filling will leak out during baking. Brush the edges with egg wash, cream, or water and they'll adhere better when you press them together. Crimping the edges with a fork is extra insurance that they will hold.

You also need to cut vents in free-form pies before baking. Otherwise, the filling will steam, and because the steam is trapped inside, the top crust will lift away from the bottom, causing a leak. Use the tip of a sharp knife to cut little slashes or poke holes in the top of each pie.

Fillings

Only a handful of the fillings in this book are heated during assembly. Warm fillings will turn any pie dough into a soggy mess, making it hard to handle. So if you do make a warm filling, be sure to let it cool before you fill the pastry. Fillings for free-form pies should not be too wet, because this will result in leaky pies. Relatively juicy fillings are fine for structured pies or jar pies because the juice will be trapped in the container instead of running all over your baking sheet, plus the dough has the extra support of the tin or jar during baking.

Finely chopped fillings work nicely in hand pies because they cook uniformly. Large slices of fruit cook unevenly, and are often difficult to cover with dough, which must be stretched to accommodate chunky pieces. For fillings where the fruit is sliced, cut thin slices and make them as uniform as possible.

Cooking

All assembled pies should be refrigerated for at least 30 minutes before they go into the oven or into hot oil. This helps keep the pastry flaky and intact (warm pastry tends to shift and leak). Most pies are done—whether baked or fried—when their crusts are golden.

You can fully blind bake the crusts for structured pies or jar pies. Preheat the oven to 375°F/190°C/gas 5 unless otherwise directed. Line each pastry-lined jar or muffin-tin cup with parchment paper, extending it beyond the rim, and fill with pie weights. Bake for 10 minutes. Remove from the oven, and carefully lift out the paper and the weights (these should lift easily from the pastry, without sticking). Return the jars or muffin tin to the oven and continue baking until the pastry looks dry and is golden, about 5 minutes. Crusts baked in muffin-tin cups will usually bake 2 to 3 minutes faster overall than jar-baked crusts. Remove from the oven and let cool completely on a baking rack before filling. Cooled blind-baked crusts can be carefully removed from their baking containers and kept in an airtight container at room temperature for up to 2 days before filling. Some pies call for a partially baked crust, such as the Pumpkin Pie on page 63. In this case, the crust is ready for filling after the parchment and weights have been removed and the crust has cooled completely. Once the crust is filled, it is returned to the oven to finish baking.

Visual cues have been included in the recipes to avoid over- or underbaking. Times are provided too, of course, but because your oven may run hotter or colder than the test oven, the times should be regarded as guides only. Your eyes, nose, and sometimes touch are the surest tools to judge doneness.

Freezing
You can freeze your pies before you bake them and the crust will still come out flaky and the filling juicy. Wrap them individually in plastic wrap, place in a resealable plastic bag, and freeze for up to 3 months. Jar pies can be frozen in the jar, baked or unbaked; simply screw on the lid. (Some of the jar pies in this book cannot be frozen, which is indicated in the relevant recipes.) They will keep for up to 2 months. Free-form, structured, and jar pies (remember to remove the lid) can go straight from the freezer into a hot oven, usually preheated to 375°F/190°C/gas 5, unless otherwise indicated in individual recipes.

Using Prepared Dough

We all need a shortcut sometimes, especially when we want to avoid a floury mess on a busy weeknight. Luckily, a number of prepared doughs on the market work well for handheld pies.

Many excellent crusts, including those with lard, are available from bakeries and other purveyors. For example, both Flying Pigs Farm, a regular at the New York City Greenmarket, and Prather Ranch, a shop in the San Francisco Ferry Building, sell excellent ready-made lard pie crusts. Ask at farm stands, Amish markets, and gourmet shops and you may be surprised by how many great crust options you'll find. Local pizza parlors will also often sell lumps of pizza dough that can be used for amazing sweet or savory small pies. (A pizza-crust pocket filled with Nutella and baked at 500°F/260°C is transcendent!)

We have also experimented with lots of different brands of prepared dough available at our local supermarkets, some of which are good. You should do the same to find the best ones in your area. Pepperidge Farm makes a good puff pastry, and Dufour produces a superb product. (It also sells a chocolate puff pastry dough, if you can find it!) To date, we have not found a widely available prepared pie crust that tastes as good as homemade.

If you buy frozen dough from a supermarket or other source, it will need at least 2 hours at room temperature or at least 4 hours in the refrigerator to thaw. No matter how tempted you might be to try it, do not microwave frozen dough so it is ready sooner. You'll end up with some sticky, partially baked goo.

Working with Pizza Dough

Pizza dough is naturally springy and spongy, which means you cannot roll it out or gather up and reroll the scraps as you can with pastry dough. It cannot be cut with cookie cutters, either. The good news is, pizza dough is very forgiving stuff. Tear it? Pinch it back together. Need a little stretch to contain a mound of filling? When gently handled, it will stretch without ripping.

The easiest way to "roll out" pizza dough is to pick it up and stretch it with well-floured knuckles and the backs of your hands, moving your hands in a counterclockwise motion, the same way you've seen pizza makers do it in the movies. You can also roll it with a rolling pin, but it will constantly shrink back at the edges, so be prepared for it to be slow going if you opt for the pin.

Remember to use a little cornmeal on your baking sheet for an authentic pizza flavor for your savory pies.

How to Fry Pies

I was skeptical about fried pies because frying is messy. An oily haze hangs in the air of your kitchen. I don't like to clean the stove top or the frying pan afterward, and I inevitably struggle over how to dispose of the dirty oil. So when Rachel insisted that we had to fry pies for this book, I reluctantly agreed, then procrastinated endlessly.

Finally, I had no choice: the manuscript was due. Up against the deadline, I was forced to fry pies. I dragged my cast-iron frying pan from a low cupboard, glugged in some oil, and set my burner to high.

For my first batch, I'd built my pies from Flaky Butter Crust (page 108) and Peach Filling (page 127). Thinking I'd much rather be loading a baking tray into my oven, I lowered three pies into the hot oil. They were seized immediately by bubbling fat; they hissed and browned in less than a minute. I turned them quickly and carefully, and the second side browned in equal time. Using a slotted spoon, I scooped them from the oil onto a plate lined with several layers of paper towels, where they glistened, golden and crisp.

I allowed the steam to subside, then I raised one to my lips. And, whoa! The crust shattered pleasingly against my teeth. The filling, hot and sweet, oozed just enough that I had to lick warm fruit from my lips. These were amazing! I quickly devoured all three and realized I was converted.

The Way

Line a plate or rimmed baking sheet with paper towels. Pour oil to a depth of 1½ to 2 in/4 to 5 cm in a large, deep, heavy frying pan (at least 10 in/25 cm in diameter). Set the pan over high heat and heat the oil until it registers 365°F/185°C on a deep-frying thermometer. This may take up to 10 minutes. If you don't have a thermometer, shake a few drops of water or drop a bead or two of dough into the oil. If they sizzle on contact, the oil is ready.

Add three or four pies to the hot oil and fry, turning them once, until golden, about 1 minute on each side. If the oil gets too hot—you will know if this happens because the pies will darken too quickly—lower the heat to medium-high. Using a slotted spoon or wire skimmer, transfer the pies to the paper towel–lined plate to drain. Serve the pies warm. Fried pies don't keep well, so eat them the day you fry them.

Choosing a crust

Use the Flaky Butter Crust (page 108), Sturdy Cream Cheese Crust (page 117), or Luscious Lard Crust (page 110). The Versatile Cornmeal Crust (page 114) is more fragile than the others, and if you fry the pies a few seconds too long, the crust takes on an acrid flavor.

Choosing a filling

One rule applies: Because you don't want leakage or flavorlessness, your filling should not be too wet or too dry. With the exception of the custards, mousses, and mashed potato fillings in the jar pies chapter, any filling in this book will make a fine fried pie. Dried apple and raisin (see page 129) is traditional, as are raspberry (see page 125), apricot or peach (see page 127), or pecan fillings (see page 55). The mozzarella, tomato, and prosciutto filling (see page 39) is absolutely sublime when fried—a tangy, salty, gooey tangle in a fried shell.

Shaping, filling, and sealing the pies

Keep the shape of your pies simple, such as half-moons or triangles. Don't try to load too much filling into each pie. You don't want to have to stretch the dough over the filling. Instead, the dough should fold easily, with the filling neatly encased inside. A folded edge is much stronger than a sealed edge, so you need to seal the open edges securely. Brush the pastry edges with water or beaten egg, pinch them together firmly, and then crimp them with a fork for added strength, if you like.

Choosing an oil

Use a clean-tasting vegetable oil, such as canola, corn, or grapeseed. Olive oil will work, too, but it contributes a specific flavor that may work beautifully with some fillings (savory, peach, apricot) but clash with or overpower others (apple, berry). It also has a lower smoke point than the other oils; if it overheats, it can impart an off taste to your pies. You can use lard, too. It sounds decadent, but it fries cleanly.

Leaky pies

If a pie leaks, the filling may burn and flavor the oil. Use a slotted spoon or wire skimmer to fish the fried bits of fruit or other filling ingredients and crust crumbs from the oil before frying a new batch of pies.

Finishing fried pies

For just a little more flavor to lick from your fingers, toss hot sweet fried pies in cinnamon sugar (½ cup/ 100 g sugar mixed with 2 tsp ground cinnamon) or sprinkle hot savory pies with fine sea salt.

Profile: *Mamaw's Fried Pies*

Whitehouse, Texas | *co-owners* Nell Hoce and Sandra Harvell

The story of Mamaw's fried pies is less about its namesake—though Mamaw was surely a skilled producer of peach, apple, and apricot pockets—than the tale of her twin daughters, Nell Hoce and Sandra Harvell. A pair of energetic redheads who don't look a day over fifty or act a second over thirty (though they got their Medicare cards in 2010), they have pretty much always done everything in tandem. "We tell people we share one brain," jokes Sandra, "so we have to stick together." It's nearly true. Not only do they run their perpetually packed Whitehouse, Texas, bakery and restaurant side by side, but their husbands are best friends, too. In fact, in the early 1980s, the foursome moved together from Houston to Whitehouse, a tiny northeast Texas town—population just seven thousand—next door to much larger Tyler.

The sisters had worked as manicurists in Houston for fifteen years, and although they knew they were ready to give up painting nails, they weren't ready to sit still. They decided to try frying up the little picture-perfect half-moon pies they had made growing up in the small community of Adger, Alabama. They started at state fairs and festivals, working from a red truck painted with a white sign that said MAMAW'S, the nickname given to their mother by her grandchildren. When Sandra and Nell were children, their mother would make fried hand pies for them, their three sisters, and their brother, using fruits that grew "at the home place," as Sandra calls their old Alabama property. Mamaw taught her daughters how to mix, roll out, fill, and shape the dough—crimping the edges with a fork—and how to fry up the

pies in deep iron frying pans. "I remember it as if it were yesterday," says Sandra.

She also remembers how to make what she insists is the key to their wildly successful business: Mamaw's pie crusts. "You could open a canned filling and put it on her pie crust and it would taste wonderful," says Sandra. "She didn't use Crisco. Crisco doesn't work. We have to use lard." That's about as much as they'll tell you, however. Give up their recipe? "Girl, I can't do that," teases Sandra, "that's the secret to our success."

Whatever they do, it works. Sandra and Nell quickly found fame with their fried pies, outgrowing their little red truck as word spread of their cooking skills, first with rave reviews in local newspapers and then through a profile on the popular *Texas Country Reporter* television show. Jobs catering parties and events streamed in, so they expanded to a bigger commercial kitchen. But they quickly outpaced that, too, and opened a storefront complete with a screen door in 2008. They have since moved to a spacious shop near Tyler, on Texas State Highway 110.

"It's just been phenomenal," says Sandra of the response to their positive press. Luckily, their current space can seat hundreds for catered dinners of their legendary pies if need be—and yes, the need does arise—and boasts an enormous central kitchen that's "state of the art," says Sandra. The kitchen is open for all to see five days a week from 8:00 A.M. to 4:00 P.M., during which a whopping four hundred to six hundred pies are made daily.

For the most part, the cooks still follow Mamaw's instructions—"Everything is done by hand," says

Sandra—though everything is now done on a much larger scale. Instead of filling the pockets with only peach, apple, or apricot, as the sisters did in Alabama, Mamaw's offers twenty-eight flavors, from potato, egg and cheese, meat, and chicken to mincemeat, pecan, pineapple, Bing cherry, chocolate, coconut, German chocolate, lemon, and nearly anything else you can think of, except for sweet potato. "We had trouble finding good sweet potatoes," explains Sandra, who says her favorite filling these days is blackberry, served with a scoop of ice cream.

They've adjusted the recipe from a cup of this and a third of a cup of that to sixteen cups of this and five cups of that, and instead of mixing the ingredients in stainless-steel bowls, the flour and lard are kneaded each morning by Herbert and Ron—"our husbands make the dough for us," explains Sandra—with help from a massive stand mixer. The cast-iron frying pans full of hot oil are gone too, replaced by six big commercial deep fryers. The only way to make the pies is to fry the pies, insists Sandra. "You can't bake a fried pie," she says. "We've tried. Bake a pie, and it's dry."

Meanwhile, a team of eight help Sandra and Nell roll out the dough, and the sisters have recently ceded the responsibility of shaping the pies to two Mexican American women who grew up making tortillas by hand. They apply their skills and dexterity to filling and forming hundreds of pies a day using only their fingers and a small mold. "They make more pies than my sister and I could ever make in a day," raves Sandra.

That, of course, gives the sisters more time to play with fillings and flavors and to tinker with their menu. They've added a hot-plate lunch service to their take-out pie shop, making sell-out specialties like meat loaf and mashed potatoes, chicken fried steak, fried chicken, grilled chicken salad with pecans and mandarin oranges, chicken and dumplings, pinto beans, fried okra, and BLTs.

Serving hundreds of folks a square meal and a blackberry pie is taxing, and you would think that instead of adding to their workload as they move deeper into their sixties, these ladies would be stepping back a bit. Not a chance. "We work so hard," says Sandra of their efforts to steadily improve the Mamaw's menu, "that it would be hard to give it up."

Of course, she means not only their peach and lemon hand pies or their fried chicken, but also their dedicated customers. "It's really amazing; people are just so nice to us," says Sandra. "It's been a lovely ride. Two little country girls—we never could have dreamed of it."

MAMAW'S FRIED PIES, *1010 State Highway 110 North, Whitehouse, Texas; (903) 871-8100; www.mamawsfriedpies.com*

chapter one FREE-

FORM

PIES

Welcome to the wonderful world of cutting, shaping, filling, and sealing dough. These are the pie-making techniques you will learn in this chapter, the building blocks for making simple, delightful handheld pies.

WHAT IS A FREE-FORM PIE?

A free-form pie is what you most likely picture when you hear the words *handheld pie*. Free-form pies are composed of a top and bottom crust, folded over or sealed together at the edges. They can be square, round, triangular, star shaped, heart shaped, or the shape of the pie mold you are using. We invented the category to describe the pie-making techniques outlined in this chapter, just as the term *structured pies* describes a different set of techniques in the following chapter.

Think of empanadas; they are, by our definition, free-form pies. So is the pop tart, the nostalgic rectangular breakfast pastry. Our homemade pop tarts—we include three delicious recipes here—are not too sweet, our flavors are both classic and adult, and the genre is kicked up a notch by using bright-flavored ingredients and baking the pies. These treats were made to be eaten out of hand, on the go, and we had to tackle our own versions not only because pie is an ideal breakfast, but also because pop tarts epitomize the concept of a handheld pie!

All of the recipes in this chapter belong here because they represent the ideal marriage of crust shape and filling consistency. The fillings are sturdy and intense enough to stand up to a greater crust surface area, which means you can make these pies larger than any other type of pie in the book. Don't make them too big, however. If the surface area is too large, the pies will crumble and break if you truly intend to eat them out of hand. They should never be larger than 5 in/12 cm, and they are most successful at 4 in/10 cm.

If you're filling free-form pies, you'll want to make the pieces of fruit as small as possible so you can get the maximum amount of filling into each pie. A plump, whole cherry takes up a lot of space in a little pie! So we halve, quarter, slice, grate, dice, or mash fruits in the fillings in the Nuts and Bolts chapter. You can also grind the fruits to a chunky purée in a food processor, or you can shred fruits such as pears and apples on the large holes of a box grater or in a food processor fitted with the shredding blade. The ratio of fruit to sugar will be the same regardless of how small you cut the fruit.

It is also important that the filling not be too soupy. That's why fillings that lean toward creamy or custardy, such as a pumpkin or a cheese filling, are used in structured pies, Chapter 2, where the crust has the support of a muffin-tin cup.

This chapter will have a special place in the hearts of crust worshippers: there is twice as much crust as filling in a free-form pie.

Free-Form Pie Master Recipe

makes 12 to 32 pies, depending on size

½ recipe Flaky Butter Crust (page 108), Sturdy Cream Cheese Crust (page 117), Luscious Lard Crust (page 110), or Versatile Cornmeal Crust (page 114)

All-purpose flour for dusting

1 recipe any filling in Nuts and Bolts chapter

1 egg, lightly beaten, or 3 tbsp heavy cream

Sugar for sprinkling (optional)

1. Line two rimmed baking sheets with parchment paper. Remove the dough from the refrigerator.

2. Lightly flour a clean work surface. Unwrap the dough, place it on the floured work surface, and flour the top lightly. Roll out the dough into a large square or a circle about ⅛ in/3 mm thick. It should measure 12 to 14 in/30.5 to 35.5 cm. Using a sharp knife, a fluted or plain pastry wheel, a biscuit or cookie cutter, or a pie mold, cut the dough into the desired shape, creating as many cutouts as possible. Any shape will work, as long as it can be folded over onto itself and the edges match up, such as square into a triangle or rectangle, a circle into a half-moon, and so on. Gather up the dough scraps, form into a ball, roll out, and cut out more pieces. (Reroll the dough only once or it will bake up tough.)

3. The simplest free-form pie is made by cutting out squares, placing a small mound of filling in the center of each square, folding the square in half, and adhering the edges. You can fold the pies on a clean countertop, or you can cup a dough square in one hand, press the filling into the middle of the pastry, and then turn the edges of the dough up with your other hand and pinch the edges to seal.

4. Here are directions for shaping a variety of free-form pies:

    TO MAKE ROUND PIES, *cut out an even number of 2-, 3-, 4-, or 5-in/ 5-, 7.5-, 10-, or 12-cm circles. Use one circle as the bottom crust, top it with filling, fit the other circle over the filling, and then seal the edge.*

    TO MAKE HALF-MOON PIES, *cut out 4- to 10-in/10- to 25-cm circles. Fold in half over the filling to form 2- to 5-in/5- to 12-cm half-moons.*

    TO MAKE RECTANGULAR PIES, *cut out 4- to 10-in/10- to 25-cm squares. Fold in half over the filling to form 2- to 5-in/5- to 12-cm rectangles.*

TO MAKE TRIANGULAR PIES, *cut out 4- to 10-in/10- to 25-cm squares. Fold in half over the filling, point to point, to form 2- to 5-in/5- to 12-cm triangles.*

TO MAKE SQUARE PIES *(or rectangular pies from two pieces of dough), follow the directions for round pies, using squares in place of the circles.*

5. Fill each pie with 1 tsp to 3 tbsp filling, depending on size. If you are folding the dough, place the filling in the middle of the dough shape, leaving a ¼-in/6-mm border uncovered around the perimeter, and fold so the edges meet. If you are pairing matching dough shapes, place the filling in the middle of the bottom shape, leaving a ¼-in/6-mm border, and place the second piece on top. Moisten the edges of the dough with the beaten egg, and press them together to form a secure seal. You can use the tines of a fork to crimp the edges as well. Refrigerate the shaped pies for at least 30 minutes or up to 24 hours before baking. Preheat the oven to 375°F/190°C/gas 5.

6. Just before baking, arrange the pies, spacing them about 1 in/2.5 cm apart, on baking sheets. Brush them with the beaten egg and sprinkle with a little sugar, if you like.

7. Place the trays in the oven and bake the pies until the crust is golden, 15 to 20 minutes. Remove from the oven and carefully move the pies to a baking rack to cool for at least 15 minutes before serving.

The baked pies can be kept in an airtight container at room temperature for up to 2 days or frozen for up to 2 months. Reheat in a 375°F/190°C/gas 5 oven for about 12 minutes.

Chocolate-Cinnamon Pop Tarts

makes about 16 pop tarts

1 recipe Flaky Butter
Crust (page 108)

1 cup/200 g sugar

2 tsp ground cinnamon

1 egg

1 tbsp cold water

All-purpose flour
for dusting

1 recipe Bittersweet
Ganache Filling
(page 134), at room
temperature

I am a big fan of chocolate in the morning, in its many exquisite forms: *pain au chocolat*, hot chocolate crowned with cream, Nutella spread on grainy toast. Every part of this pop tart—the good smear of bittersweet chocolate, the flaky buttery pastry that encases it—approximates the flavor and texture of a chocolate croissant.

1. Make the dough, form each half into a rough rectangle, and chill as directed.

2. Preheat the oven to 375°F/190°C/gas 5. Line two rimmed baking sheets with parchment paper.

3. In a small bowl, stir together the sugar and cinnamon. In another small bowl, whisk together the egg and water. Lightly flour a clean work surface. Remove half of the dough from the refrigerator, unwrap it, place it on the floured work surface, and flour the top lightly. Roll out the dough into a rectangle that measures roughly 9 by 12 in/ 23 by 30.5 cm. It should be about ⅛ in/3 mm thick.

4. Using a plain or fluted pastry wheel, trim off the ragged edges. Then cut the dough into neat 3-by-2-in/7.5-by-5-cm rectangles, saving the trimmings. (If you're like me, your pieces won't be identical, so when you go to fill the tarts, you'll want to eyeball the rectangles and match up those closest to the same size.)

5. Transfer half of the rectangles to a prepared baking sheet, spacing them about 1 in/2.5 cm apart. These are the "bottoms." Spoon 1 tbsp of the ganache onto each rectangle, leaving ¼ in/6 mm of the edge uncovered on all sides. Top the ganache with 1 tsp of the cinnamon sugar. Using a brush or your finger, dampen the edge of the rectangle with the egg wash. Carefully place a second rectangle on top of the first, and press to seal the edges together. Repeat with the remaining rectangles, then crimp the edges with the tines of a fork. Using the

fork tines, puncture the top layer of the pastry a few times. Sprinkle with 2 to 3 tbsp of the remaining cinnamon-sugar mixture. Refrigerate, uncovered, for at least 15 minutes or up to 2 hours. Repeat the rolling, cutting, filling, and crimping with the second half of the dough. Gather the dough scraps from both halves, form into a ball, and roll out to make a few more pastries. (Reroll the dough only once or it will bake up tough.) You should have about 16 pop tarts total.

6. When the second baking sheet of pies is ready, remove the first pan from the refrigerator, and sprinkle any remaining cinnamon sugar over the pastries on both baking sheets. Place the first pan in the oven and the second in the refrigerator, and then place a baking rack over a sheet of parchment on your table or counter. (This saves the surface from sticky drips!) Bake the pastries until they are golden brown on top (the sides will brown first), about 20 minutes.

7. Remove from the oven and immediately (and carefully) move the pastries onto the baking rack, then slip the second baking sheet into the oven. Let the pastries cool for at least 30 minutes before serving.

The fully cooled baked pies can be kept in an airtight container at room temperature for up to 2 days or frozen for up to 3 months. Reheat in a 375°F/190°C/gas 5 oven for about 12 minutes before serving.

Peanut Butter and Jelly Pop Tarts

makes about 16 pop tarts

1 recipe Flaky Butter
Crust (page 108) or
Sturdy Cream Cheese
Crust (page 117)

1 egg

1 tbsp cold water

All-purpose flour
for dusting

1 cup/280 g creamy
peanut butter

¾ cup/215 g Concord
Grape Filling (page 119)
or jam of choice

Pop tarts are great with a variety of different fillings, especially chocolate or any berry or apple. But I have weakness for this peanut butter and jelly combo. If you are a crunchy peanut butter person, you can substitute it for the creamy kind, though I find that the flaky crust is all the texture I need. For a nostalgic flavor and look, sprinkle the pop tarts with a little colored sugar before they go in the oven, or brush a simple glaze (recipe follows) on the fully cooled pop tarts.

1. Make the dough, form each half into a rough rectangle, and chill as directed.

2. Preheat the oven to 375°F/190°C/gas 5. Line two rimmed baking sheets with parchment paper.

3. In a small bowl, whisk together the egg and water. Lightly flour a clean work surface. Remove half of the dough from the refrigerator, unwrap it, place it on the floured work surface, and flour the top lightly. Roll out the dough into a rectangle that measures roughly 9 by 12 in/ 23 by 30.5 cm. It should be about ⅛ in/3 mm thick.

4. Using a plain or fluted pastry wheel, trim off the ragged edges. Then cut the dough into neat 3-by-2-in/7.5-by-5-cm rectangles, saving the trimmings. (If you're like me, your pieces won't be identical, so when you go to fill the tarts, you'll want to eyeball the rectangles and match up those closest to the same size.)

5. Transfer half of the rectangles to a prepared baking sheet, spacing them about 1 in/2.5 cm apart. These are the "bottoms." Gently spread each one with 1 tbsp of the peanut butter, starting from the center and stopping within ¼ in/6 mm of the edge on all sides. Top the peanut butter with 2 tsp of the grape filling. Using a brush or your finger, dampen the edge of the rectangle with the egg wash. Carefully place a second rectangle on top of the first, and press to seal the edges

together. Repeat with the remaining rectangles, then crimp the edges with the tines of a fork. Using the fork tines, puncture the top layer of the pastry a few times. Refrigerate, uncovered, for at least 30 minutes or up to 2 hours. Repeat the rolling, cutting, filling, and crimping with the second half of the dough. Gather the dough scraps from both halves, form into a ball, and roll out to make a few more pastries. (Reroll the dough only once or it will bake up tough.) You should have about 16 pop tarts total.

6. When the second baking sheet of pop tarts is ready, place the first pan in the oven and the second in the refrigerator, and then place a baking rack over a sheet of parchment on your table or counter. (This saves the surface from sticky drips!) Bake the pastries until they are golden brown on top (the sides will brown first), about 20 minutes.

7. Remove from the oven and immediately (and carefully) move the pastries onto the baking rack, then slip the second baking sheet into the oven. Let the pastries cool for at least 30 minutes before serving.

The fully cooled baked pies can be kept in an airtight container at room temperature for up to 2 days or frozen for up to 3 months. Reheat in a 375°F/190°C/gas 5 oven for about 12 minutes.

Confectioners' Sugar Glaze

In a bowl, combine 2 cups/200 g confectioners' sugar, 4 tsp whole milk, and 1 tbsp fresh lemon juice and stir until smooth. If the mixture is too thick to spread, add a little more milk. Makes about ⅔ cup/165 ml.

Profile: *Whiffies*

Portland, Oregon | *founder and chief fryer* Gregg Abbott

Ask many young bakers today why they chose to cast aside a more traditional career path in favor of cooking for a living and the common refrain is that they were looking for an old-fashioned sense of kinship and community, for a way to put smiles on people's faces by satisfying their bellies. All of that is true for Gregg Abbott, owner of Whiffies fried-pie truck in Portland, Oregon, but for him it was even more personal. "Damn," he said to himself a few years back, when he was working as a valet in downtown Portland, "I can't go on parking cars two nights a week and being a total bum."

Ironically, it was another downtown Portland parking lot that he says saved his soul. That's the lot at SE Twelfth Avenue and Hawthorne Boulevard, now known as Cartopia. For the past decade, from lunch break until nearly daybreak, this food truck court has been full of *al asphalto* diners munching some of the city's best snacks, like the gravy, curd, and French-fry dish called *poutine* from Potato Champion, or the wood-fired San Marzano tomato–topped pizzas from Pyro. And now there is Whiffies Fried Pies, where Gregg, with help from his sister, Summer, serves a slew of golden-fried crescents filled with an ever-changing roster of goodies—Oregon marionberries, coconut cream and smoked almonds, cherry chocolate chip, peanut butter cream, chicken, Kahlúa pork, barbecued beef and cheese (always a favorite)— from midday until 3:00 A.M.

Like most other Portlanders under forty, Gregg spent plenty of time at Cartopia before he launched Whiffies. "I fell in love with the lot," he says. "To me, this was what Portland is all about—this cool, late-night hangout." He became friendly with some

of the vendors, like Mike McKinnon, who runs Potato Champion, and soon decided that what he wanted to do with his life was sell food from a truck in a parking lot. "I didn't have the capital or the skill to own a restaurant," Gregg remembered thinking, "but I figured I could run a food cart."

Most of us would get quizzical smiles from our parents if we told them we wanted to operate a food truck. But Gregg's father is "a world-class chef," as Gregg puts it, used to working "psychotic sixteen-hour days and not thinking that's abnormal," and his mother is a marketing consultant. Together they run a catering business in Portland. But more important, years earlier they operated a little business in Maui making dinner on the beach for honeymooners and the like, doing it with nothing but "two burners and a cooler full of food," says Gregg. "It was minimalist," he adds. In other words, they understood what Gregg wanted to do.

So with help from his parents and a little capital from a "sort of real-estate deal" he had made in 2006, Gregg was able to buy a used food truck from its fourth owner, who had used its oven primarily to heat pizzas. "I gutted the thing," he says, "and built it out like a tiny commercial kitchen."

Meanwhile, he was perfecting his fried pies. The decision to make fried pies over, say, meatballs or Indian *dosas* was due to three carefully considered criteria. First, he knew he wanted something that could be eaten out of hand while standing alongside the truck. Second, he wanted something classic, something traditional, something "that was almost fairlike." And third, he wanted something different from what was already available citywide. Fried pies were the answer.

As it turns out, Gregg knew something about the concept. "I grew up with pie in my life," he says. He recalls making them with his German American grandparents, who lived in Pennsylvania. "They were delicious pies, and I was so small I had to stand on a stool to peel the apples and peaches." He started testing his recipes—both sweet and savory—in his parents' commercial catering kitchen, enlisting his father's advice on his efforts.

"My father was stuck on the idea that we would bake these pies," says Gregg, who would give out samples of each batch to the kitchen workers. "The baked hand pies were good," Gregg says, "but something was missing. I could just see that it wasn't getting the results I wanted." Gregg pushed for plunging a batch of the pies into the deep fryer. His father didn't think it was a good idea, but eventually told him to "do what you need to do," recalls Gregg. "The tasters had already each eaten maybe five and a half pies," he says. "They were like 'oh, I don't want any more pies.'" But when he fried up a batch and handed them out, he could tell by the looks on their faces that frying was what had been missing.

The public soon agreed. Even before the truck was in service, Gregg's Twitter stream was the talk of all the chowhounders in town. Now his pies sell out well before he closes up for the night, and they have been written up in nearly every publication in Portland. One local food blogger even describes Portland life in terms of the iconic pies: "There was a time before the Whiffies fried-pie cart opened, and then there's everything after." (The name Whiffies is a family joke, a nickname Gregg's dad gave to both Gregg and Summer. It is also used as an all-purpose word for something trivial. It's doubly funny now, as neither the business nor the pies are remotely lightweights.)

These days Gregg has a commercial space and employees to help prepare the fillings—many vegan friendly; a few created as guest pies by local chefs—and a sheeter to help roll out the shortening-based dough. (Gregg favors shortening over butter because the pastry fries up extra flaky, and butter burns in the oil of the deep fryer.) The sheeter, he insists, is less about increasing production than it is about relieving some of the physical stress of rolling out hundreds of pies. In 2009, he and his sister were making all the fillings right in the tiny truck and using a wooden pie former handmade in rural Canada to fold the pies. But that was for "church ladies to make one hundred of them a week," says Gregg. "It was not made to turn out one hundred to two hundred pies a day."

That he'd be making that many, and in such a short time span, is amazing, a fact not lost on Gregg: "It's crazy how quickly it went. I got into this trend at exactly the right moment," he says of both food trucks and old-fashioned American comfort food. "It was sheer luck." Whatever the reasons for his success, he can be sure of one thing: he is not a bum, even if he does spend his days and nights in a parking lot.

WHIFFIES, SE Twelfth Avenue and Hawthorne Boulevard, Portland, Oregon; (503) 946-6544; www.whiffies.com

Orange Marmalade–
Mascarpone Pop Tarts
makes about 16 pop tarts

I love marmalade for breakfast: spooned over yogurt, stirred into oatmeal, spread on buttered toast. I wondered how it would fare as a pop tart filling, and the verdict is in—very nicely! But the marmalade tastes best when paired with a creamy cheese, so I've put them together here. You can also substitute other preserves for the marmalade; sour cherry jam is especially good.

1. Make the dough, form each half into a rough rectangle, and chill as directed.

2. Preheat the oven to 375°F/190°C/gas 5. Line two rimmed baking sheets with parchment paper.

3. In a small bowl, whisk together the egg and water. Lightly flour a clean work surface. Remove half of the dough from the refrigerator, unwrap it, place it on the floured work surface, and flour the top lightly. Roll out the dough into a rectangle that measures roughly 9 by 12 in/23 by 30.5 cm. It should be about ⅛ in/3 mm thick.

4. Using a plain or fluted pastry wheel, trim off the ragged edges. Then cut the dough into neat 3-by-2-in/7.5-by-5-cm rectangles, saving the trimmings. (If you're like me, your pieces won't be identical, so when you go to fill the tarts, you'll want to eyeball the rectangles and match up those closest to the same size.)

5. Transfer half of the rectangles to a prepared baking sheet, spacing them about 1 in/2.5 cm apart. These are the "bottoms." Gently brush each rectangle with 1 tbsp of the mascarpone, starting from the center and stopping within ¼ in/6 mm of the edge on all sides. Top the cheese with 2 tsp of the marmalade. Using a brush or your finger, dampen the edge of the rectangle with the egg wash. Carefully place a second rectangle on top of the first, and press to seal the edges together. Repeat with the remaining rectangles, then crimp the edges

CONTINUED ⟶

1 recipe Flaky Butter Crust (page 108) or Sturdy Cream Cheese Crust (page 117)

1 egg

1 tbsp cold water

All-purpose flour for dusting

1 cup/225 g mascarpone or cream cheese

¾ cup/215 g orange marmalade

with the tines of a fork. Using the fork tines, puncture the top layer of the pastry a few times. Refrigerate, uncovered, for at least 15 minutes or up to 2 hours. Repeat the rolling, cutting, filling, and crimping with the second half of the dough. Gather the dough scraps from both halves, form into a ball, and roll out to make a few more pastries. (Reroll the dough only once or it will bake up tough.) You should have about 16 pop tarts total.

6. When the second baking sheet of pop tarts is ready, place the first pan in the oven and the second in the refrigerator, and then place a baking rack over a sheet of parchment on your table or counter. (This saves the surface from sticky drips!) Bake the pastries until they are golden brown on top (the sides will brown first), about 20 minutes.

7. Remove from the oven and immediately (and carefully) move the pastries onto the baking rack, then slip the second baking sheet into the oven. Let the pastries cool for at least 30 minutes before serving.

The fully cooled baked pies can be kept in an airtight container at room temperature for up to 24 hours or frozen for up to 3 months. Reheat in a 375°F/190°C/gas 5 oven for about 12 minutes.

Mozzarella, Tomato, and Prosciutto Pie

makes twelve to sixteen 2- to 6-in/5- to 15-cm pies

This recipe works beautifully with any crust in this book. But you can also skip making the dough from scratch and use prepared pizza dough for an easy calzone-like treat. This basic formula can be jazzed up with other ingredients, too. For example, add a scattering of finely diced red bell pepper; a smear of tapenade or Calabrian chile paste; two or three paper-thin garlic slices; a pinch of minced fresh sage, oregano, or rosemary; or a sprinkle of grated Parmesan or Pecorino Romano cheese to each pie.

1 recipe Flaky Butter Crust (page 108), Luscious Lard Crust (page 110), Sturdy Cream Cheese Crust (page 117), Versatile Cornmeal Crust (page 114), or 8 oz/225 g prepared pizza dough (see page 19)

All-purpose flour for dusting

6 to 8 oz/170 to 225 g fresh mozzarella cheese, thinly sliced

3 plum tomatoes, thinly sliced

3 slices prosciutto, cut into narrow strips

10 large fresh basil leaves, cut into narrow strips

1. Make the dough as directed, form each half into a rough rectangle, and chill as directed. Or, have the pizza dough on hand.

2. Preheat the oven to 375°F/190°C/gas 5. Line two rimmed baking sheets with parchment paper.

3. Lightly flour a clean work surface. Remove half of the dough from the refrigerator, unwrap it, place it on the floured work surface, and flour the top lightly. Roll out the dough into a rectangle that measures roughly 9 by 12 in/23 by 30.5 cm. It should be about ⅛ in/3 mm thick.

4. Using a plain or fluted pastry wheel, trim off the ragged edges. Then cut the dough into circles, squares, or rectangles, as small or as large as you like (make sure they are big enough to enclose the cheese and tomato slices), saving the trimmings. Read the directions in the Free-Form Pie Master Recipe (page 28) on how to fold or cap the shape you have chosen, then, using about half each of the cheese, tomatoes, prosciutto, and basil, fill and shape the pies, sealing the edges and crimping decoratively, if you like. (Or, you can fill and shape as directed for any of the pop tarts on pages 30 to 37.) Slash or prick each pie to vent steam.

CONTINUED ⟶

5. Transfer the pies to a prepared baking sheet, spacing them about 1 in/ 2.5 cm apart. Refrigerate, uncovered, for at least 15 minutes or up to 2 hours. Repeat the rolling, cutting, filling, and crimping with the second half of the dough. Gather the dough scraps from both halves, form into a ball, and roll out to make a few more pastries. (Reroll the dough only once or it will bake up tough.)

6. When the second baking sheet of pies is ready, place the first pan in the oven and the second in the refrigerator, and then place a baking rack over a sheet of parchment on your table or counter. (This saves the surface from sticky drips!) Bake the pastries until they are golden brown on top (the sides will brown first), about 20 minutes.

7. Remove from the oven and immediately (and carefully) move the pastries onto the baking rack, then slip the second baking sheet into the oven. Let the pastries cool for at least 10 minutes before serving or you risk a hot-cheese burn on the roof of your mouth!

The fully cooled baked pies can be kept in an airtight container at room temperature for up to 24 hours or frozen for up to 2 months. Reheat in a 375°F/190°C/gas 5 oven for about 12 minutes.

Chicken Chile Relleno Pie from Oh my! Pocket Pies, Houston, Texas

makes twelve to sixteen 2- to 6-in/5- to 15-cm pies

There is now a San Francisco fan base for this pie. I tested and tweaked the recipe given to us by the folks at Oh my! Pocket Pies, producing multiple batches that I shared with friends. The response was amazing: these pies got the loudest cheers of any pie in this book. I heard about how many pies were scarfed at one sitting, and of wives hiding the pies from their husbands. My own marriage was tested when, in a new-baby fog, I put a tray of these pies in the oven, fell asleep on the couch, and burned a batch. Whoops. This mistake is invoked every time I put a pie in the oven. So keep your eyes on these pies! I encourage you to make extra: not only are they delicious, but the finished pies freeze beautifully. For an even greater treat, dip them into sour cream or *pico de gallo*. They can also be fried, following the directions on page 20.

2 tbsp canola oil

1 small yellow onion, diced

2 garlic cloves, minced

1 lb/455 g ground chicken

½ cup/85 g fresh or frozen corn kernels (if frozen, do not thaw)

Salt

Freshly ground pepper, preferably white

2 tbsp unsalted butter

½ cup/65 g all-purpose flour, plus more for dusting

2 tsp ancho chile powder or New Mexico chile powder

½ tsp sweet paprika

⅛ tsp ground cumin

¼ tsp dried oregano

1 cup/240 ml water

2 or 3 poblano chiles, roasted, peeled, seeded, and chopped

3 oz/85 g Monterey Jack cheese, shredded

2 tsp fresh lime juice

1 recipe Flaky Butter Crust (page 108), Luscious Lard Crust (page 110), Sturdy Cream Cheese Crust (page 117), or Versatile Cornmeal Crust (page 114)

1. In a large frying pan, warm 1 tbsp of the canola oil over medium heat. Add half of the onion and cook, stirring occasionally, until softened, about 5 minutes. Add the garlic and stir until fragrant, about 1 minute. Add chicken and cook, breaking it up with a wooden spoon or spatula and stirring occasionally, until opaque, about 10 minutes. Add the corn and cook until just tender, about 3 minutes. Season with salt and pepper. Pour the mixture into a large bowl and set aside.

2. Return the frying pan to medium heat and add the remaining 1 tbsp oil. When it is hot, add the remaining onion and cook, stirring occasionally, until softened, about 5 minutes. Add the butter and let it melt. Then add the flour and stir until it coats the onion evenly. Cook, stirring frequently, until the flour begins to turn golden, about 5 minutes. Stir in the chile powder, paprika, cumin, and oregano and cook, stirring, for 1 minute. Increase the heat to medium-high and gradually add the water, stirring constantly, until the mixture thickens to the consistency of a gravy,

CONTINUED ⟶

about 5 minutes. Pour the onion mixture into the chicken mixture and let cool for 10 minutes. Mix in the chiles, cheese, and lime juice, then taste and adjust the seasoning. Let cool completely. (The mixture can be stored in an airtight container in the refrigerator for up to 2 days before continuing.)

3. Preheat the oven to 375°F/190°C/gas 5. Line two rimmed baking sheets with parchment paper.

4. Lightly flour a clean work surface. Remove half of the dough from the refrigerator, unwrap it, place it on the floured work surface, and flour the top lightly. Roll out the dough into a rectangle that is roughly 9 by 12 in/23 by 30.5 cm. The dough should be about ⅛ in/3 mm thick.

5. Using a plain or fluted pastry wheel, trim off the ragged edges. Then cut the dough into circles, squares, or rectangles, as small or as large as you like, saving the trimmings. Read the directions in the Free-Form Pie Master Recipe (page 28) on how to fold or cap the shape you have chosen, then, using 1 tbsp filling in each pie, fill and shape the pies, sealing the edges and crimping decoratively, if you like. (Or, you can fill and shape as directed for any of the pop tarts on pages 30 to 37.) Slash or prick each pie to vent steam.

6. Transfer the pies to the prepared baking sheet, spacing them about 1 in/2.5 cm apart. Refrigerate, uncovered, for at least 30 minutes or up to 2 hours. Repeat the rolling, cutting, filling, and crimping with the second half of the dough. Gather the dough scraps from both halves, form into a ball, and roll out to make a few more pastries. (Reroll the dough only once or it will bake up tough.)

7. When the second baking sheet of pies is ready, place the first pan in the oven and the second in the refrigerator, and then place a baking rack over a sheet of parchment on your table or counter. (This saves the surface from sticky drips!) Bake the pastries until they are golden brown on top (the sides will brown first), about 20 minutes.

8. Remove from the oven and immediately (and carefully) move the pastries onto the baking rack, then slip the second baking sheet into the oven. Let the pastries cool for at least 10 minutes before serving, but be sure to enjoy them warm.

Eat or freeze these pies the day they are made. They can be frozen for up to 2 months. Reheat in a 375°F/190°C/gas 5 oven for about 12 minutes.

Profile: *Oh My! Pocket Pies*

Houston, Texas | *owners* Joe Phillips and Joanna Torok

At first glance, you might think that Oh my! Pocket Pies, a fried-pie truck in Houston, Texas, is just another fast-food fix. For starters, there's that silly name and the convenience-food-friendly menu: fluffy-crusted pies filled with Salisbury steak; cheesy squash casserole; peanut butter and jelly; marshmallows, graham crackers, and Nutella (in honor of the s'more); and, this being the Lone Star State, spicy chicken chile relleno. "If you live in Houston," explains Joe Phillips, who runs the operation with help from his longstanding girlfriend, Joanna Torok, "you need chicken chile relleno." Plus, there's the retro aesthetic of the place, a nod to a time when plastics were perfection and packaged foods were not just easy, but cutting edge. Even the truck's Web site features drawings of fresh-faced folks with *Leave It to Beaver* looks.

Joe admits that Oh my! Pocket Pies owes some of its inspiration to TV dinners. "When I was a kid, both of my parents worked, and one of my fondest memories is of eating Swanson's chicken potpies and watching kung fu movies on the tube." But this farm-sourced hand-pie bakery business, which was launched in 2009, is much more about substance than style. Unlike those frozen potpies that Joe grew up eating, Oh my! treats are made with love and care and garden-fresh vegetables, just like Grandma's. In fact, Joe chose the name for his business not just to make people smile—it usually does—but also because of the response his homemade pies so often elicit: "Oh my! This tastes like what my grandmother used to make."

Just like a grandma-run operation, Joe and Joanna are the only employees, though Joanna still works a day job as operations manager for the Houston Grand Opera. Together, they manage all the details, from the truck's Twitter feed (it is how Houstonites find this 100 percent mobile operation) to frying three hundred pies for a catered event to ringing up dozens of orders for chicken chile relleno pockets during the daily lunch rush. "We wear several hats and adapt to the environment," says Joanna with a laugh. "And we don't mind scrubbing floors." Nor, apparently, do they mind upper-body workouts: "We roll everything out by hand," says Joe, who has noticed that the daily chore of forming balls of dough and rolling them out has affected his physique. "Joe has a Popeye arm," Joanna says of his right bicep, now larger than the left.

Joe and Joanna are just as serious about using local products as they are about doing the work themselves. This attitude stems in part from Joe's background as a marketing consultant for small local restaurants in Austin. He often advised those struggling to succeed to set themselves apart from their competition by working with local producers. The goal was not only to serve fresher, better-tasting food, but also to build community and to put money back into the local economy.

"Keep it local," Joe would tell his Austin clients, and that same philosophy drives Oh my! Pocket Pies today. For example, Joe and Joanna buy many of their vegetables, fruits, and herbs at Houston's Highland Village farmers' market, which means they serve seasonal specials, like roasted sweet potato pie in September or strawberry pie in spring. That passion for supporting local vendors is captured in the Oh my! Pocket Pies blog, where Joe and Joanna talk about the produce from Atkinson Farms, Lynn Walker's Gulf Coast shrimp, or the beef raised by cattleman Ray Law. "Where would our Salisbury steak be without the Beef Boss?" the couple once enthused online. They also dispense their culinary wisdom right from the truck, where, along with a twice-baked potato pie, they'll give you a quick spiel about the guy who grew the potatoes.

Joe's pocket-pie business started when he tried to make his own versions of store-bought foods, like those frozen potpies he ate in front of the TV. "I made my own gravy," Joe says of his first attempts to take control of his cravings. "If you buy frozen dinners at the grocery store, they taste like crap," he says, "and I don't know what I'm eating."

His cooking experiments soon extended to the smile-shaped Argentine beef pies he had been introduced to while working at The Empanada Parlour in Austin, the town where he and Joanna met and lived before moving to Houston. ("I couldn't get rid of him," she wryly recalls.) One night, he made a batch from scratch. "I thought they were delicious," Joanna remembers, "all eggs and olives and ground beef." So when Joe finally decided to start his own business, those little Argentine pockets, fried in peanut oil, ended up on the menu, along with a few burgers, a garden salad, sun tea brewed daily in the Texas rays, and hand-cut fries. There's no better food product to serve from a cart than a handheld meal, insists Joanna, "and we can stuff lots of ingredients into those little carriers."

The mobile makeup of their business—they cruise Houston daily and post their location online—was also carefully thought out. Joe's days as a consultant taught him that a food cart would be a wise first step. A truck, he says, is a far less expensive way to grow a customer base than a bricks-and-mortar restaurant is. And back in 2009, food trucks, with the exception of the city's longstanding taco trucks, were just becoming a Houston trend.

Even with the dozens of regulars who love tracking the whereabouts of the truck and its fried pies online, the pair admits that one day they hope to own a place with a real address and real seating, rather than a Twitter feed and a street-side bench. But despite the literal road ahead and the long hours, both Joe and Joanna feel pretty darn good whenever customers express their joy after a bite of a chicken chile relleno pie. "You can feel that little bit of sunshine on the back of your neck," he says, "and it's all worth it."

OH MY! POCKET PIES, on the streets of Houston, Texas; www.ohmypocketpies.com

chapter two

STRUCTURED
— PIES —

R   R

The pies in this chapter, which we have dubbed *structured pies*, rely on a pan to hold their shape while they bake. We use standard muffin tins to form tiny pies that can be finished in four or five bites, showcasing a greater proportion of filling to crust than the other pies in this book. In terms of filling-to-crust ratio, structured pies are the opposite of free-form pies: there's twice as much filling as crust in a structured pie. For those of you who love your fruit more than your pastry, or relish the sensation of biting through a tall, warm pumpkin custard cradled in a buttery crust, this is the pie shape for you.

H

W

MORE TO LOVE PER BITE.

Simply put, a structured pie is a classic pie made miniature. In this chapter, we feature two toothsome custards, Buttermilk-Whiskey Pie (page 58) and Pumpkin Pie (page 63). The inspiration for the quichelike Bacon, Egg, and Cheese Breakfast Pie (page 70) comes from a pie Sarah enjoyed during a snowy stay in a Quebecois B & B. It is guaranteed to stick to your ribs on cold mornings but also makes a delicious dinner paired with a crunchy green salad. The diminutive Pecan Pie (page 55) delivers more toasty, sweet nuts with less syrupy goo than a full-sized pecan pie.

If you need to transport these pies, keep them in their baking tins, or slip them into muffin papers. For charming fluted edges, bake structured pies in tiny tart pans or brioche molds; for deeper pies, use popover pans. You may need to adjust the baking time slightly to accommodate a larger or smaller baking-cup size, in which case, look for golden edges on your pastry and other visual cues specified in the individual recipes.

Many of these recipes use only a half recipe of dough, which means you can get two batches of pies from each batch of dough. And if you are a novice pie baker, you'll be happy to know that structured pies are more forgiving than free-form pies. They're much easier to shape and handle. If you're inexperienced at handling pastry, you can just pat pieces of dough into muffin cups. The pies will still bake up beautifully.

Structured Pie Master Recipe

makes 12 to 16 pies

You don't need to butter the muffin-tin cups; your pies will pop right out. Be careful not to overfill the crusts, however, or the filling may leak and cause the pie to stick to the cup. You also don't need to fully blind bake the crust for any of the recipes in this chapter, though you do need to partially blind bake the crust for the Pumpkin Pie (page 63). If you come up with your own recipe for these little structured pies and want to blind bake the crusts, follow the instructions on page 18.

½ recipe Flaky Butter Crust (page 108), Luscious Lard Crust (page 110), Sturdy Cream Cheese Crust (page 117), or Versatile Cornmeal Crust (page 114)

All-purpose flour for dusting

1 recipe any filling in Nuts and Bolts chapter

1 egg (optional)

Sugar for sprinkling (optional)

1. Have two 12-cup standard muffin tins ready. Remove the dough from the refrigerator.

2. Lightly flour a clean work surface. Unwrap the dough, place it on the floured work surface, and flour the top lightly. Roll out the dough into a circle about ⅛ in/3 mm thick. It will be about 14 in/35.5 cm in diameter. Using a round biscuit or cookie cutter, cut out as many circles 4 in/ 10 cm in diameter as possible.

3. Handling the dough circles gently, lift each circle and press it into a muffin cup, leaving a ⅛- to ¼-in/3- to 6-mm overhang and patching any tears by pinching them together or plugging them with a dough scrap. You can crimp the dough that extends beyond the edge of the cup with fork tines or your fingers so it adheres to the top of the tin and forms a rim, if you like, but it is not necessary. Gather the dough scraps, form into a ball, roll out, and cut out more circles. (Reroll the dough only once or it will bake up tough.) You should have 12 to 16 circles total. If you don't have enough dough circles to fill every cup in a muffin tin, stagger the crusts rather than clustering all of them at one end of the tin. If you've filled one muffin tin, refrigerate it while you line the cups in a second tin.

4. If you want to make double-crust pies, cut out 4-in/10-cm circles for the bottom crusts and an equal number of 3-in/7.5-cm circles for the top crusts.

CONTINUED ⟶

If you want to add a lattice top to your pies, use a plain or fluted pastry wheel to cut any leftover dough into strips ¼ in/6 mm wide. Or, cut out small leaf, heart, circle, or other shapes with very small cookie cutters. Refrigerate the strips or cutouts until you are ready to assemble the pies.

5. Place 3 to 4 tbsp filling in each cup. If you are adding a decorative element, such as a lattice top, a cutout, or a top crust, add it now. To form a lattice, lay three parallel strips across the filling; each strip should touch the opposite edges of the cup. Fold half of the middle strip back. Lay one strip perpendicular to the first three strips, positioning it across the middle of the pie, then unfold the middle strip over it. Pick up both ends of each of the two remaining strips on the pie and fold them toward the middle of the pie. Lay two more strips perpendicular to the first strips, then unfold the ends of the folded strips, laying them over the added strips. To top the pies with decorative cutouts, carefully lay the cutouts on top of the filling. To make double-crust pies, lay the 3-in/7.5-cm circles over the filling, gently press the edges of the dough circles together, and cut a small slash or poke holes in the top of each pie with a sharp knife tip or the tines of a fork. Refrigerate the assembled pies for at least 30 minutes or up to 24 hours. Preheat the oven to 375°F/190°C/gas 5.

6. If you have topped the pies with a decorative element or a top crust, just before baking, in a small bowl, whisk the egg until blended. Lightly brush the lattice, the cutouts, or the top crust with the egg, then sprinkle with sugar, if you like.

7. Bake the pies until the filling is set and the crust is golden brown, about 20 minutes.

8. Let cool on a baking rack for at least 1 hour before serving. Run a sharp, thin knife around the edge of each pie to loosen it from the cup. Then, using the knife tip or a fork, gently pry each pie upward so you can grab it with your fingertips and lift it out of the tin. Serve warm or at room temperature.

    The baked fruit pies can be kept in an airtight container at room temperature for up to 2 days or frozen for up to 2 months. Reheat in a 375°F/190°C/gas 5 oven for 10 to 12 minutes. Follow the instructions in individual recipes for storing other pies.

Pecan Pie

makes 12 to 16 pies

To me, pecans are the sweetest and softest of nuts. There's something quite decadent and dessert-y about them; I shudder when I see them in savory applications. This reaction, I think, stems from my love of gooey, nutty pecan pie. If you want to gild the lily, drizzle the top of each pie with melted chocolate, or put a pat of Bittersweet Ganache Filling (page 134) at the bottom of the cup for a delicious surprise. These pies can also be made in jars; follow the Double-Crust Jar Pie Master Recipe on page 76.

1. Have two 12-cup standard muffin tins ready. Remove the dough from the refrigerator.

2. Lightly flour a clean work surface. Unwrap the dough, place it on the floured work surface, and flour the top lightly. Roll out the dough into a large circle about ⅛ in/3 mm thick. It will be about 14 in/35.5 cm in diameter. Using a round biscuit or cookie cutter, cut out as many circles 4 to 5 in/10 to 12 cm in diameter as possible.

3. Handling the dough circles gently, lift each circle and press it into a muffin cup, leaving a ⅛- to ¼-in/3- to 6-mm overhang and patching any tears by pinching them together or plugging them with a dough scrap. You can crimp the dough that extends beyond the edge of the cup with fork tines or your fingers so it adheres to the top of the tin and forms a rim, if you like, but it is not necessary. Gather the dough scraps, form into a ball, roll out, and cut out more circles. (Reroll the dough only once or it will bake up tough.) You should have 12 to 16 circles total. If you don't have enough dough circles to fill every cup in a muffin tin, stagger the crusts rather than clustering all of them at one end of the tin. If you've filled one tin, refrigerate it while you line the cups in a second tin, then refrigerate the second tin.

½ recipe Flaky Butter Crust (page 108), Luscious Lard Crust (page 110), or Sturdy Cream Cheese Crust (page 117)

All-purpose flour for dusting

2 eggs

½ cup/100 g firmly packed light or dark brown sugar

½ cup/120 ml corn syrup or blackstrap molasses

1 tbsp bourbon (optional)

1 tsp grated orange zest (optional)

1 tsp vanilla extract

½ tsp kosher salt

2 cups/225 g pecans, coarsely chopped

CONTINUED ⟶

4. In a bowl, whisk together the eggs, brown sugar, and corn syrup until light in color. Whisk in the bourbon and orange zest (if using) and then whisk in the vanilla and salt. Stir in the pecans.

5. Remove the dough-lined cups from the refrigerator. Fill each cup two-thirds full with the pecan mixture. Refrigerate the assembled pies for 30 minutes. Preheat the oven to 350°F/180°C/gas 4.

6. Bake the pies until the filling is golden brown and no longer jiggles when tapped, about 15 minutes.

7. Let cool on a baking rack for at least 1 hour before serving. Run a sharp, thin knife around the edge of each pie to loosen it from the cup. Then, using the knife tip or a fork, gently pry each pie upward so you can grab it with your fingertips and lift it out of the tin. Serve warm or at room temperature.

   The pies can be kept in an airtight container at room temperature for up to 3 days or frozen for up to 2 months. Reheat in a 350°F/180°C/gas 4 oven for about 5 to 7 minutes.

Buttermilk-Whiskey Pie

makes 12 to 16 pies

½ recipe Flaky Butter
Crust (page 108) or
Luscious Lard Crust
(page 110)

All-purpose flour
for dusting

4 eggs

1½ cups/360 ml
buttermilk

¾ cup/150 g firmly
packed light brown
sugar

½ cup/115 g unsalted
butter, melted

3 tbsp whiskey or
bourbon (optional)

1 tsp vanilla extract

Freshly grated nutmeg
for sprinkling (optional)

My first bite of buttermilk pie was a warm, gooey custard that was so sweet it made my teeth ache. There was something about it I liked, and a lot that I didn't. I know that buttermilk pie is supposed to be sweet as it can be, but I decided that although I liked the tang and milkiness of the buttermilk, I wanted less sweetness. So I have restructured this classic and given it a whiskey kick. If you don't care for the oh-so-slight booziness of these babies, you can replace the spirit with 1 tsp grated lemon zest. These pies can also be made in jars; follow the instructions for Banana Cream Pie on page 78.

1. Have two 12-cup standard muffin tins ready. Remove the dough from the refrigerator.

2. Lightly flour a clean work surface. Unwrap the dough, place it on the floured work surface, and flour the top lightly. Roll out the dough into a large circle about ⅛ in/3 mm thick. It will be about 14 in/35.5 cm in diameter. Using a round biscuit or cookie cutter, cut out as many circles 4 to 5 in/10 to 12 cm in diameter as possible.

3. Handling the dough circles gently, lift each circle and press it into a muffin cup, leaving a ⅛- to ¼-in/3- to 6-mm overhang and patching any tears by pinching them together or plugging them with a dough scrap. You can crimp the dough that extends beyond the edge of the cup with fork tines or your fingers so it adheres to the top of the tin and forms a rim, if you like, but it is not necessary. Gather the dough scraps, form into a ball, roll out, and cut out more circles. (Reroll the dough only once or it will bake up tough.) You should have 12 to 16 circles total. If you don't have enough dough circles to fill every cup in a muffin tin, stagger the crusts rather than clustering all of them at one end of the tin. If you've filled one tin, refrigerate it while you line the cups in a second tin, then refrigerate the second tin.

4. In a bowl, whisk the eggs until blended. Add the buttermilk, brown sugar, butter, whiskey (if using), and vanilla and whisk until smooth.

5. Remove the dough-lined cups from the refrigerator. Fill each cup two-thirds full with the buttermilk mixture. Refrigerate the assembled pies for 30 minutes. Preheat the oven to 350°F/180°C/gas 4.

6. Bake the pies until the filling is slightly puffed and lightly browned, about 20 minutes. The filling should jiggle slightly when a tin is gently shaken.

7. Let cool on a baking rack for 45 minutes before serving. Run a sharp, thin knife around the edge of each pie to loosen it from the cup. Then, using the knife tip or a fork, gently pry each pie upward so you can grab it with your fingertips and lift it out of the tin. Sprinkle the tops of the pies with nutmeg, if desired. Serve warm or at room temperature.

   The pies can be kept in an airtight container at room temperature for up to 2 days. Reheat in a 350°F/180°C/gas 4 oven for 5 to 7 minutes. This pie cannot be frozen.

Profile: *The BitterSweet Bakery*

St. Louis, Missouri | *co-owner and baker Leanna Russo*

There's a squeaky screen door at The BitterSweet Bakery in St. Louis, and it's there on purpose, explains owner Leanna Russo. It's supposed to remind you of your grandparents' house. "That's what the bakery is about," says Leanna. "People come in for a memory," for a taste of their past.

At BitterSweet—the full name is The BitterSweet Bakery, a Sweet Boutique—you won't find guar gum, anything done "extreme," or cupcakes with electric blue frosting. What you will find are beautiful old-fashioned layer cakes, apple crumb tarts, blueberry–brown butter muffins, house-made strawberry jams and tiny bagels, biscuits and gravy and eggs, biscotti and peach ice cream, Concord grape pie, peanut butter shortbread, chantilly cream pie, and, of course, fresh fruit–filled hand pies, all made from scratch.

"I didn't grow up eating things out of a box," says Leanna, who opened the shop with help from her husband, Kurt, in the early weeks of 2010. "Our mentality is to get back to grandma and to get away from contrived crazy desserts."

Plenty of folks talk up getting back to basics, back to the baking and canning traditions of their forbears. But in this case, it's not just talk. Leanna grew up in an Amish farming community in rural Ohio, where good food was a blessing, the garden stood in for the grocery store, some neighbors were electricity free, and pickling was a necessity, not a pastime. In fact, one of the strongest food memories from her childhood is of baking hand pies with her great-grandmother Ida. "She seemed like she was eighty when I was born," jokes Leanna, "and as far as I can tell, she always lived right next door."

Leanna fills her hand pies with tart cherries or other seasonal fruits, but her great-grandmother always filled her hand pies with tart-sweet apples, lightly crimped the pastry edges with a fork, cut a small steam vent in the top, and then baked them until golden brown, or about ten minutes longer than when you think they are done. During the fall apple harvest, Leanna remembers, "we would always make hand-pie filling and we would make applesauce." The pastry dough was fashioned according to Ida's hand-measuring method, a method that Leanna continues to use. "It was two handfuls of flour, one handful of fat, and a pinch of salt," says Leanna. The method still works, even though today's handfuls are dramatically different. "My great-grandmother," she laughs, "had midget-size hands."

Despite those memories, baking was the last thing Leanna wanted to do when she first went to culinary school. "I eat like a man," she told the St. Louis *RiverFront Times* when her shop first opened, noting a particular passion for cassoulet and duck confit. "I think you would be most surprised at what I don't eat: sugar and sweets," she confessed to a reporter.

"I got my first restaurant job when I was eleven years old," Leanna recalls, "and pastry always seemed like the most boring part of the kitchen work." That changed when she was assigned to a pastry department as part of her school externship and things didn't always go well. She found herself obsessing over why some desserts went wrong and how to fix them. All of a sudden, she says, she had gone to "the dark side," as she jokingly calls dessert. She may not technically love it now, she adds, but that's okay. "Your passion has to consume you, and I constantly wonder why things go wrong. It's basically a love-hate relationship." That explains the name BitterSweet, too.

Leanna's résumé is as impressive as her complicated passion. There's her childhood on a farm, a degree from the Napa Valley Cooking School in Northern California, and time in the kitchen of Chicago's Trio restaurant, which consistently ranked as one of the nation's finest dining rooms in the early 2000s. But she counts a stint back home in Ohio in the late 1990s, after culinary school, as even more influential to her current philosophy. She went to work at a specialty bakery called Pistachio, where she discovered the Chef's Garden, one of the first organic vegetable farms to cater to restaurants. In those days, before the popularity of farm-to-table food, a pastry chef having access to high-quality farm-fresh ingredients was relatively rare. Working with the Chef's Garden reinforced what Leanna already knew from her childhood: her family cooked from the farm, using what was fresh and seasonal, because that was what was available.

That approach is seen in everything made at BitterSweet. The hand pies, based on her great-grandmother's recipe, are filled with blackberries in spring, peaches in summer, and apples in fall. Leanna is quick to point out that she can't always source locally, however. "We never claim to be local or organic," she says. "We just claim to use good ingredients."

She also has good help from Kurt, who, says Leanna, doesn't make any of the sweets—"I can't remember him ever cooking anything . . . maybe spaghetti?"—but who has "the most amazing palate. He could eat sweets all day." He also helps take care of their young daughter, who spends her days with her parents at the bakery. She was born the month it opened and was named after the sweetest holiday of all: she is called Valentine.

THE BITTERSWEET BAKERY, *2200 Gravios Avenue, St. Louis, Missouri; 314-771-3500; www.thebittersweetbakery.com*

Pumpkin Pie
makes 12 to 16 pies

What more is there to say about pumpkin pie? It seems to be the favorite pie of every third person I meet. It is the only pie my husband bakes. But for me, it is ho-hum. I'd rather eat just about any other kind of pie, unless I'm craving spices, in which case pumpkin is the way to go. Sweet pumpkin filling makes a star of cinnamon like few other substances on Earth. And this filling is especially good with any nut butter crust variation (see Sarah's Take on Flavored Crusts, page 109). These pies can also be made in jars; follow the Double-Crust Jar Pie Master Recipe on page 76.

½ recipe Flaky Butter Crust (page 108), Luscious Lard Crust (page 110), or Sturdy Cream Cheese Crust (page 117)

All-purpose flour for dusting

One 15-oz/430-g can unsweetened pumpkin purée (about 2 cups)

3 eggs

1 cup/200 g firmly packed light brown sugar

⅓ cup/75 ml whole milk or buttermilk

⅔ cup/165 ml sour cream or crème fraîche

2 tbsp unsalted butter, melted

2 tsp vanilla extract

2 tsp ground cinnamon

1 tsp ground ginger

¼ tsp freshly grated nutmeg

Pinch of kosher salt

1. Have two 12-cup standard muffin tins ready. Remove the dough from the refrigerator.

2. Lightly flour a clean work surface. Unwrap the dough, place it on the floured work surface, and flour the top lightly. Roll out the dough into a large circle about ⅛ in/3 mm thick. It will be about 14 in/35.5 cm in diameter. Using a round biscuit or cookie cutter, cut out as many circles 4 to 5 in/10 to 12 cm in diameter as possible.

3. Handling the dough circles gently, lift each circle and press it into a muffin cup, leaving a ⅛- to ¼-in/3- to 6-mm overhang and patching any tears by pinching them together or plugging them with a dough scrap. You can crimp the dough that extends beyond the edge of the cup with fork tines or your fingers so it adheres to the top of the tin and forms a rim, if you like, but it is not necessary. Gather the dough scraps, form into a ball, roll out, and cut out more circles. (Reroll the dough only once or it will bake up tough.) You should have 12 to 16 circles total. If you don't have enough dough circles to fill every cup in a muffin tin, stagger the crusts rather than clustering all of them at one end of the tin. If you've filled one tin, refrigerate it while you line the cups in a second tin, then refrigerate the second tin. Refrigerate the lined cups for 30 minutes. Preheat the oven to 400°F/200°C/gas 6.

CONTINUED ⟶

4. Remove the dough-lined cups from the refrigerator. Line each cup with parchment paper, extending it beyond the rim, and fill with pie weights. Place in oven, and bake until the pastry is pale gold, about 10 minutes. Remove from the oven and place on a baking rack. Remove the weights and parchment and let the crusts cool for at least 15 minutes before filling.

5. In a bowl, whisk together the pumpkin, eggs, brown sugar, milk, sour cream, butter, vanilla, cinnamon, ginger, nutmeg, and salt until smooth. Fill each cooled pastry cup two-thirds full with the pumpkin mixture.

6. Bake in the oven for 10 minutes. Reduce the oven temperature to 325°F/165°C/gas 3 and continue to bake until the tip of a sharp knife inserted into the center of a pie comes out clean, 12 to 15 minutes longer. The pies are ready if the filling jiggles slightly when a tin is gently shaken.

7. Let cool completely in the tin(s) on a baking rack, at least 2 hours. The pies should easily lift from the cups when cool. Use a knife tip or fork to pry each pie gently upward so you can grab it with your fingertips and lift it out of the tin. Serve at room temperature.

The pies can be kept in an airtight container at room temperature for up to 2 days or frozen for up to 2 months. Reheat in a 350°F/180°C/gas 4 oven for about 10 minutes.

Farmer Cheese Pie from Four & Twenty Blackbirds, Brooklyn, New York

makes 12 to 16 pies

This pie is one of Rachel's favorites from Four & Twenty Blackbirds in Brooklyn. Straightforward yet sophisticated, it is the perfect combination of hearty cheese, subtle herb, and gentle honey. It makes a wonderful hors d'oeuvre or lunch pie and is especially good when paired with a cornmeal crust, as I have done here, though a butter or lard crust (see pages 108 and 110, respectively) is an excellent choice, too. The filling puffs as it bakes and becomes a lovely light gold. If you cannot find farmer cheese, ricotta cheese or cottage cheese can be substituted (see variation). These pies can also be made in jars; follow the Double-Crust Jar Pie Master Recipe on page 76.

½ recipe Versatile Cornmeal Crust (page 114)

All-purpose flour for dusting

1⅔ cups/380 g farmer cheese

3 eggs

½ cup/120 ml half-and-half

3 tbsp honey

Pinch of kosher salt

1 to 2 tbsp fresh thyme leaves

1. Have two 12-cup standard muffin tins ready. Remove the dough from the refrigerator.

2. Lightly flour a clean work surface. Unwrap the dough, place it on the floured work surface, and flour the top lightly. Roll out the dough into a large circle about ⅛ in/3 mm thick. It will be about 14 in/35.5 cm in diameter. Using a round biscuit or cookie cutter, cut out as many circles 4 to 5 in/10 to 12 cm in diameter as possible.

3. Handling the dough circles gently, lift each circle and press it into a muffin cup, leaving a ⅛- to ¼-in/3- to 6-mm overhang and patching any tears by pinching them together or plugging them with a dough scrap. You can crimp the dough that extends beyond the edge of the cup with fork tines or your fingers so it adheres to the top of the tin and forms a rim, if you like, but it is not necessary. Gather the dough scraps, form into a ball, roll out, and cut out more circles. (Reroll the dough only once or it will bake up tough.) You should have 12 to 16 circles total. If you don't have enough dough circles to fill every cup in a muffin tin, stagger the crusts rather than clustering all of them at one end of the tin. If you've filled one tin, refrigerate it while you line the cups in a second tin, then refrigerate the second tin.

CONTINUED →

4. In a stand mixer fitted with the paddle attachment, beat together the cheese and eggs until smooth. Add the half-and-half, honey, and salt and beat until thoroughly combined. (Or, use a large bowl and a handheld mixer or a wooden spoon.) Generously sprinkle in the thyme and stir to mix. (The filling can be made up to 24 hours in advance and refrigerated.)

5. Remove the dough-lined cups from the refrigerator. Place 3 to 4 tbsp filling in each cup. Refrigerate the assembled pies for at least 30 minutes or up to 24 hours. Preheat the oven to 375°F/190°C/gas 5.

6. Bake the pies until the filling is slightly puffed and golden, about 20 minutes. The filling should jiggle slightly when a tin is gently shaken. Be careful not to overbake or the filling will crack.

7. Let cool on a baking rack for 10 minutes. Run a sharp, thin knife around the edge of each pie to loosen it from the cup. Then, using the knife tip or a fork, gently pry each pie upward so you can grab it with your fingertips and lift it out of the tin. Serve warm or at room temperature.

The pies can be kept in an airtight container at room temperature for up to 2 days or frozen for up to 2 months. Reheat in a 375°F/190°C/gas 5 oven for about 10 minutes before serving.

Ricotta Cheese or Cottage Cheese Variation

Substitute ricotta or cottage cheese in the same amount for the farmer cheese. Scoop into a sieve placed over a bowl and drain in the refrigerator for 2 hours before using.

Profile: *Four & Twenty Blackbirds*

Brooklyn, New York | *co-owners* Emily and Melissa Elsen

It was probably inevitable that Emily and Melissa Elsen, the twenty-something sisters who run Brooklyn's Four & Twenty Blackbirds café, would end up baking. For starters, their father is a wheat farmer near the small town—just four hundred souls—of Hecla, South Dakota, where the girls grew up, and his harvests go into baked goods around the country. Also, as youngsters, Emily and Melissa worked at the Calico Kitchen, a family-style restaurant in Hecla where their mother, Mary, and her sisters served three squares a day from 1985 to 2001. Grandmother Liz, who was already well into her seventies, helped out, too, turning out trays of cinnamon buns, soft white rolls, and nearly thirty different kinds of pie—the most coveted were sour cream raisin and coconut cream—almost every day.

"The girls always did like cookbooks," Mary says of her daughters. "I let the kitchen be a free place for them. But creating food, creating something good to give to people," she adds, "that was in their blood."

Emily and Melissa didn't plan on launching their own sibling-run restaurant when they first got out of school. "I never wanted to clean another deep-fat fryer," says Melissa, recalling her years in Calico's busy kitchen. Maybe that's why she studied business and finance at college, after Emily, two years Melissa's senior, studied art. Both traveled after school, and then Emily ended up in Brooklyn, where she worked at the farmers' market and eventually opened an art gallery and studio space in an up-and-coming New York City neighborhood called Gowanus. Melissa eventually settled in Brooklyn, too.

The sisters ended up sharing both an apartment and a hobby, baking. Grandma Liz's lessons at Calico had made an impression. She had taught the girls not just the basics of baking, but also the perfect touch with their all-butter crusts (which they still make by hand daily at the café). Even though from the start their creations—chile chocolate, salted honey, grapefruit custard, cranberry sage—were decidedly more modern than Grandma Liz's, they were declared just as delicious. "Everybody seemed to love them," says Emily of the baked goods they would deliver to friends. "It was like we had given them gold."

In their spare time, the sisters started selling their sweet pies and tarts and savory hand pies (stuffed with curried potato apple or cheese) to friends, and they began to cater parties, including a few at the gallery where Emily worked. Word of their short-crust skills soon spread. Then, when a corner space nearly perfect for a pie shop became available near Emily's gallery, the sisters told their parents they wanted to open a café and pie shop and asked for their help.

Mary was skeptical at first, and with good reason. "Are you sure you want to go that route?" she remembers asking her daughters, warning them of what she knew from her own experience. "You never get a day off." But Emily and Melissa persisted, so their parents helped them secure a loan from a South Dakota bank, and the entire family, led by a talented carpenter friend, went to work on the Brooklyn building. "Those girls were dirty from head to toe," beams Mary with pride.

That dirty work was worth it. The shop opened in 2010, and today it is a lovely space—the original pressed tinwork and rustic wooden floor were preserved—where regulars happily spend hours at a table or lined up at the door waiting for a space to open. The small, open kitchen, complete with well-worn copies of Susan Gold Purdy's *As Easy as Pie* and the *Farm Journal's Complete Pie Cookbook*, is as comforting and inviting as a farmhouse kitchen. One wall is often hung with art from local artists; another is lined with windows that let in light year-round and window boxes that flourish with herbs in the warm months. (The sisters also inherited their green thumbs. Their parents' rhubarb patch is so large and grows so abundantly in South Dakota's cooler summers that their father ships the harvest across a half-dozen state lines so his daughters can use rhubarb in their pies year-round.)

The sisters serve house-made fizzy sodas, including a wonderfully tart lemon version kicked with rosemary-scented sugar and a dash of bitters; excellent coffee from a roaster in upstate New York; fresh herb–laced quiches; fat, buttery scones; and a cheesy egg custard with a buttermilk-biscuit center they call "egg in a nest." And, of course, there are plenty of pies, both full size and pocket size, that rotate on and off the menu with the seasons. Spring brings strawberry balsamic, pear Brie, mint-bourbon-chocolate, and buttermilk chess or shoofly. Come fall, you'll find honeyed pumpkin, maple buttermilk custard, and an herby farmer cheese. Salty nut and chocolate, dark chocolate and dried cherry, bittersweet chocolate with cranberries, and ruby port and roasted nuts are winter specialties. Summers are best of all: nectarine blueberry, stone-fruit crumble, peach berry, cherry, honeyed apricot, lavender, and seven types of rhubarb, including custard, honey, apple, fig, and blood orange.

All this tastes as good as it sounds, and even though Emily brushes off the sisters' smashing success as part of the Brooklyn culinary boom— "The time must've been right for it," she shrugs— Four & Twenty Blackbirds has already earned raves from the best reviewers: *Bon Appétit* magazine named it one of the top ten places for pie in America, and Martha Stewart, the country's most celebrated pie baker, hosted them on her radio show. "In retrospect," says Emily of their current careers, "why didn't we go to culinary school?" Their fans know the answer to that question: the sisters, both bakers nearly from birth, don't need any lessons.

FOUR & TWENTY BLACKBIRDS,
439 Third Avenue, Brooklyn, New York;
(718) 499-2917; birdsblack.com

Bacon, Egg, and Cheese Breakfast Pie

makes 12 pies

1 large russet potato

6 slices bacon, cut into ½-in/12-mm pieces

All-purpose flour for dusting

½ recipe Flaky Butter Crust (page 108) or Sturdy Cream Cheese Crust (page 117)

3 eggs

⅓ cup/15 g chopped fresh chives

½ cup/55 g coarsely grated aged Cheddar cheese (about 2 oz)

Although I have given you a choice of two crusts here, I recommend the Flaky Butter Crust. It puffs up a bit when it bakes, forming hot, eggy, salty pillows of early-morning deliciousness. You can assemble these pies the night before in muffin-tin cups, cover the pies with plastic wrap, refrigerate them, and then bake them in the morning (they'll need about 5 minutes longer in the oven). I like the mild flavor of the chives in this recipe, but minced yellow onion or shallot can be substituted.

1. Preheat the oven to 375°F/190°C/gas 5. Have ready a 12-cup standard muffin tin.

2. Poke holes in the potato with the tines of a fork, and bake or microwave until tender. Alternatively, peel the potato and boil until tender. Set the potato aside until it is cool enough to handle. If you have baked or microwaved the potato, split it open and fluff the interior with a fork. If you have boiled the potato, cut it into ½-in/12-mm chunks. If you have not used the oven, preheat it to 375°F/190°C/gas 5.

3. Spread the bacon pieces in a single layer on a rimmed baking sheet, place in the oven, and cook until crisp, 8 to 10 minutes. Remove from the oven and drain on paper towels.

4. While the bacon is cooking, lightly flour a clean work surface. Unwrap the dough, place it on the floured work surface, and flour the top lightly. Roll out the dough into a large circle ⅛ in/3 mm thick. You will need twelve circles 4 in/10 cm in diameter and twelve circles 3 in/7.5 cm in diameter. Using a round biscuit or cookie cutter, cut out the 4-in/10-cm circles first, then, with a 3-in/7.5-cm cutter, cut out the smaller circles. You will need to gather the dough scraps and reroll them once to cut out enough circles.

5. Handling the dough circles gently, lift the larger circles and press them into the muffin cups, patching any tears by pinching them together or plugging them with a dough scrap. Break the eggs into a measuring pitcher or a small bowl with a pouring spout and beat until combined. Divide the potato among the bottom crusts. Top the potato with the bacon pieces and chives, dividing them evenly, and then pour about 2 tsp of the beaten eggs into each muffin cup. Working quickly, top the egg with the cheese, dividing it evenly, and then with the small dough circles. Gently press the edges of the dough circles together, and cut a small slash or poke holes in the top of each pie with a sharp knife tip or the tines of a fork. Refrigerate the assembled pies for 30 minutes.

6. Bake the pies until slightly puffed and golden, about 20 minutes. Remove from the oven and let cool on a baking rack for 10 minutes. Run a sharp, thin knife around the edge of each pie to loosen it from the cup. Then, using the knife tip or a fork, gently pry each pie upward so you can grab it with your fingertips and lift it out of the tin. Serve immediately.

The pies can be kept in an airtight container at room temperature for up to 24 hours. Reheat in a 375°F/190°C/gas 5 oven for about 7 minutes. These pies cannot be frozen.

chapter three

JAR PIES

This chapter might seem out of place in a book of handheld pies, but the meringues and fluffy, creamy pies of the world deserve a place in the small-pie pantheon, and jars seem to be the perfect vessels for containing them. A jar pie can, in fact, be eaten out of hand and may prove to be the most transportable pie in your small-pie repertoire.

PLENTY DELICIOUS, AND PORTABLE.

I confess to an uncontrollable craving for cream pies and to an unhealthy fascination with the French invention *les verrines*. The latter are desserts or savory dishes composed in layers in clear-glass jars or other containers, with their beautiful strata visible through the glass. Some of these pies take after the *verrine* tradition and are meant to be spooned, such as the lovely Grasshopper Pie (page 92). Others, with both a top and bottom crust, pop right out of their jars (see Double-Crust Jar Pie Master Recipe page 76).

A number of the pies call for one of the crumb crusts in the Nuts and Bolts chapter. Because these tasty crusts are simply crumbs bound with butter, they are not sturdy enough to stand up to eating out of hand like you can a pastry crust. They do layer nicely, however, and they maintain their crunchy texture after a day or two in the refrigerator.

Most important, jar pies are little, plenty delicious, and portable. You just need to screw on the lids. Better still, they are practical. I seem to freeze everything. My family is always finding bits of cakes and other treats in my freezer. So I love nothing more than to find a way to store a pie that can be *baked later*, which is true for many jar pies: just screw the lids on tight and slip the jars in the freezer for a few weeks. This works for the Chicken Potpie (page 98), for any pies made with one of the fruit fillings in the Nuts and Bolts chapter and for the Pumpkin Pie (page 63) and Pecan Pie (page 55) in the Structured Pies chapter, if you opt to make them in jars. When you're ready to eat the pies, simply transfer them straight from the freezer to a preheated oven, and you'll have freshly baked pies in less than a half hour.

My husband says the best reason to make pies in jars is because the jars leave room for ice cream.

Tips + Techniques

Some of the pies in this chapter call for a pastry, rather than a crumb, crust, which you will have to pat into the little canning jars (see page 76). I like to roll out the dough first, cut out big squares, and press the squares into the jars, patching any holes with little nubs of dough. If you are making double-crust jar pies, remember to set aside some dough for the top crusts.

I build my pies inside the jar so the jar lid can be used. That means that the crust must never extend as high as the rim of the jar. Because the pastry will have no rim to cling to, it is critical that you chill pastry-lined jars before you blind bake them and that you weight them before they go in the oven. Otherwise, the crusts will puff and will often collapse onto themselves during baking. Refrigerate the pastry-lined jars for at least 30 minutes or up to 24 hours, then line them with parchment paper and weight them with pie weights (or dried beans). Bake them for 10 minutes in a preheated oven (usually 375°F/190°C/gas 5), then remove the weights and paper and continue baking until the crusts

are done. If that sounds too fussy, you can leave the paper and weights in place until the crusts are done.

Many of the recipes in this chapter call for only ½ recipe of a pastry crust and yield 6 pies. If you want to make 12 jar pies, double your filling recipe and use the whole pastry crust recipe. The fillings in the Nuts and Bolts chapter will double easily, as will the chocolate mousse (see page 91). If you want to make 12 pies with a custard or pudding filling, such as coconut cream (see page 80), banana cream (see page 78), or vanilla malt (see page 86), you need to make two batches of the filling, rather than double the recipe.

In most of the recipes in this chapter that call for blind baking the crusts, I have made and baked the crusts first and then made the filling. But you can usually reverse the order if you like, depending on your schedule, as many of the fillings must chill for 2 to 3 hours before they can be spooned into the crusts, giving you time to make and chill the dough and line and chill the jars.

Double-Crust Jar Pie Master Recipe
makes 8 double-crust pies

1 recipe Flaky Butter
Crust (page 108),
Luscious Lard Crust
(page 110), Sturdy
Cream Cheese
Crust (page 117), or
Versatile Cornmeal
Crust (page 114)

All-purpose flour
for dusting

1 recipe any filling
in Nuts and
Bolts chapter

1 egg

You can use any pastry recipe and any filling recipe from the Nuts and Bolts chapter to make a double-crust jar pie. These pies can be eaten right out of the jars, or you pop them out of the jars and they will be as diminutive and cute as a cupcake . . . but a pie.

In the Equipment section on page 12, I stressed how important it is to use canning jars that are wider at the mouth than at the bottom. That is especially true if you want to pop your double-crust pies out of the jars. (Of course, you can still eat them directly from the jars, too.) Straight-sided jars are also acceptable and make neater, sturdier pies.

1. Have eight ½-pt/240-ml jars ready. Remove half of the dough from the refrigerator.

2. Lightly flour a clean work surface. Unwrap the dough, place it on the floured work surface, and flour the top lightly. Roll out the dough into a square measuring 12 to 14 in/30.5 to 35.5 cm and about ⅛ in/3 mm thick. Cut the square into six uniform squares or circles. Roll out the remaining half of the dough the same way and cut out two more squares or circles of the same size and eight circles the same size as the mouth of the jar. You can flip over a jar and use it to cut these circles (it's a perfect fit!), or use a biscuit or cookie cutter. If needed, gather the dough scraps, form into a ball, roll out, and cut out more circles. (Reroll the dough only once or it will bake up tough.)

3. To line each jar, hold the jar in your nondominant hand (left hand if you are right-handed, for example) and pick up a square or circle dough in your other hand. Position the dough over the jar mouth and then gently stuff it into the jar, pressing it against the bottom and up the sides of the jar and centering it as you work. Then, using your thumbs, press the dough gently against the sides of the jar while rotating the jar slowly in a clockwise motion. Make sure the dough is clinging to the sides of the jar. It should not extend more than three-fourths of the way up the sides of the jar. Repeat to line the remaining jars.

Alternatively, carefully lift the dough round or square and fold it in half. Then, with the folded side down and the open edges facing up, lower the dough into the jar, open it, and press the dough from the middle outward to the sides of the jar.

4. Fill each pastry-lined jar with about ⅔ cup/165 ml filling. Do not fill the crusts to the top. (The jars should be no more than three-fourths full.) You want to leave at least ¼ in/6 mm of dough above the filling uncovered so you can attach the top crust. Now, lay a dough circle on top of the filling in each jar, and use your fingers or a fork to tease the edges of the crusts gently together. Cut a few small slashes in the top of each pie to allow the steam to vent. Refrigerate for at least 30 minutes or up to 24 hours. (At this point, the unbaked pies can be covered with a lid and frozen for up to 2 months.)

5. Preheat the oven to 375°F/190°C/gas 5. Just before baking, in a small bowl, whisk together the egg and 1 tbsp water until blended. Brush the top crust of each pie with the egg mixture.

6. Arrange the jars on a rimmed baking sheet, place in the oven, and bake until the top and side crusts are golden, about 25 minutes. Remove from the oven and let cool on a baking rack for at least 1 hour before serving.

7. Once the pies have cooled for 1 hour, they can be popped out of the jars. Holding a jar in your nondominant hand, run a sharp, thin knife around the inside rim of the jar with your other hand to loosen any filling that may have stuck to the glass. Then gently invert the pie into your palm. It should slide from the jar with little resistance. If it sticks, coax it out gently by running the knife along the inside edge of the jar. Once the pie slides free of the jar, quickly invert it onto a plate or the baking rack. Serve warm or at room temperature.

The baked pies can be stored in an airtight container at room temperature for up to 2 days or frozen for up to 2 months. Reheat in a 375°F/190°C/gas 5 oven for about 7 to 10 minutes.

Single-Crust Jar Pies

You can also make single-crust pies using these basic directions. Use only ½ recipe of the pastry, and omit the egg and water. Roll out the pastry as directed and cut out six uniform squares or circles. Line the jars as directed. Because you will not be adding a top crust, the dough can come up the sides of the jar. Pinch the edges against the rim and crimp them decoratively, as you would when using a pie pan or pie dish. Refrigerate as directed before baking, then fill and bake as directed until the side crusts are golden, about 25 minutes. Remove from the oven and let cool on a baking rack for at least 30 minutes before serving. Serve warm or at room temperature. Eat directly from the jar. To store the pies, screw the lids on the jars and store and reheat as directed for double-crust pies. Makes 6 single-crust pies.

Banana Cream Pie

makes 6 pies

½ recipe Flaky Butter
Crust (page 108)

3 egg yolks

2 cups/480 ml whole milk

⅔ cup/130 g granulated
sugar

¼ cup/30 g cornstarch

¼ tsp kosher salt

½ vanilla bean

2 tbsp unsalted butter

½ cup/120 ml chilled
heavy cream

1 tbsp firmly packed light
brown sugar

2 very ripe bananas

I like a salty butter crust for my banana cream pie, but you could do a delicious version with the graham cracker or chocolate crumb (see page 106; use a whole recipe of either one). Or, you can brush melted chocolate on the baked crust before you add the filling. In *Tartine*, bakers Elisabeth Prueitt and Chad Robertson suggest a thin layer of caramel between the crust and the filling that makes their pie insanely good. There is no caramel recipe in this book (though it would be an amazing addition to the apple or pear filling, too), but if you have a good caramel recipe or know a first-rate commercial caramel or butterscotch ice cream topping, go ahead and try it here. For the filling, you can use 2 tsp vanilla extract in place of the vanilla bean, but the bean contributes a richer flavor. If you're using extract, whisk it in with the butter. Make sure the bananas are very ripe. They should be heading into blackness—sweet and soft.

1. Line six ½-pt/240-ml jars with the pastry as directed for single-crust jar pies on page 77. Refrigerate for at least 30 minutes or up to 2 days.

2. Preheat the oven to 400°F/200°C/gas 6. Fit a piece of parchment paper into each pastry-lined jar, extending it beyond the rim, and fill with pie weights. Arrange the jars on a rimmed baking sheet, place in the oven, and bake for 10 minutes. Remove from the oven, lift out the weights and parchment, return the jars to the oven, and continue baking until the pastry looks dry and is golden, about 5 minutes more. Remove from the oven and let cool completely on a baking rack before filling.

3. Meanwhile, in a bowl, whisk the egg yolks until blended. Set aside. Set a fine-mesh sieve over a bowl.

4. In a saucepan, combine the milk, granulated sugar, cornstarch, and salt. Split the vanilla bean lengthwise and, using the tip of a knife, scrape the seeds into the milk mixture, then add the pod halves. Place over medium heat and cook, whisking constantly, until the mixture begins to steam and bubble at the edges of the pan, 8 to 10 minutes. Remove from the heat.

5. Gradually add about ½ cup/120 ml of the hot milk mixture to the egg yolks, whisking constantly. Pour this mixture into the saucepan while stirring constantly. Return the pan to medium heat and cook, whisking constantly, until the mixture is thickened and just beginning to bubble, about 5 minutes. Remove from the heat and whisk in the butter until melted and smooth. Strain through the sieve into the bowl. Cover with plastic wrap, pressing the wrap directly onto the surface of the mixture, and refrigerate until well chilled, at least 3 hours or up to 2 days.

6. Just before assembling the pies, in a bowl, using a whisk, whip the cream until frothy. Add the brown sugar and continue whipping until stiff peaks form. Peel the bananas and slice into thin moons.

7. Remove the pudding from the refrigerator and whisk or stir with a rubber spatula until smooth. Fold half of the banana slices into the pudding. Divide the remaining slices among the pie crusts, arranging them on the bottom. Spoon about ½ cup/120 ml of the pudding into each jar. Top the filling with a generous dollop of the whipped cream.

8. Serve immediately, or cover and refrigerate for up to 2 days, then serve chilled or at room temperature. If you smeared chocolate, caramel, or butterscotch on the crust as suggested in the headnote, let the pies rest at room temperature for 1 hour before serving to allow the coating to soften. These pies cannot be frozen.

Coconut Cream Pie

makes 6 pies

½ recipe Flaky Butter Crust (page 108)

1½ cups/170 g shredded or flaked unsweetened dried coconut

4 egg yolks

1½ cups/360 ml whole milk

1½ cups/360 ml unsweetened coconut milk

⅔ cup/130 g sugar, plus ¼ cup/50 g

5 tbsp/35 g cornstarch

¼ tsp kosher salt

1 tsp vanilla extract

1 cup/240 ml cold heavy cream

Coconut cream pie is one of my favorites. When I was little girl growing up in Pittsburgh, Pennsylvania, our family would sometimes go to a restaurant called Gullifty's, a sort of striving-to-be-high-end cosmopolitan diner with a huge rotating case of the sort of over-the-top desserts featured in trendy establishments in the 1980s. I always ordered something big and creamy, and if memory serves, it was coconut.

Decades later, I encountered a transcendent slice of coconut cream pie at Blue Plate, one of my favorite restaurants in San Francisco, and this recipe takes its cues from that adult version. The crust must possess just enough salty crunch, and the filling must be cool and creamy and include a bit of coconut flesh. The directions are for a straightforward coconut cream pie, but smearing a layer of melted chocolate on the baked crust or topping the finished pies with a scattering of chocolate shavings is not a bad idea.

Be sure to buy real-deal coconut milk, the kind that has a pad of solid cream on top. Light coconut milk simply won't deliver the same flavor or consistency to the puddinglike filling. And if you want to give the classic coconut cream pie a new frame, use 1 recipe graham cracker or chocolate crumb crust (see page 106) in place of the butter crust.

1. Line six ½-pt/240-ml jars with the pastry as directed for single-crust jar pies on page 77. Refrigerate for at least 30 minutes or up to 2 days.

2. Meanwhile, preheat the oven to 325°F/165°C/gas 3. Spread the dried coconut evenly on a rimmed baking sheet, place in the oven, and toast until golden, about 5 minutes. Once the coconut starts to brown, it can overdarken quickly, so watch closely. Remove from the oven and immediately transfer to a shallow bowl or plate and let cool completely (do not leave it on the hot pan or it will continue to brown). Increase the oven temperature to 400°F/200°C/gas 6.

CONTINUED ⟶

3. Fit a piece of parchment paper into each pastry-lined jar, extending it beyond the rim, and fill with pie weights. Arrange the jars on a rimmed baking sheet, place in the oven, and bake for 10 minutes. Remove from the oven, lift out the weights and parchment, return the jars to the oven, and continue baking until the pastry looks dry and is golden, about 5 minutes more. Remove from the oven and let cool completely on a baking rack before filling.

4. Meanwhile, in a bowl, whisk the egg yolks until blended. Set aside. Set a fine-mesh sieve over a bowl.

5. In a saucepan, whisk together the milk, coconut milk, ⅔ cup/130 g sugar, cornstarch, and salt. Place over medium heat and cook, whisking constantly, until the mixture begins to steam and bubble at the edges of the pan, 5 to 7 minutes. Remove from the heat.

6. Gradually add about ½ cup/120 ml of the hot milk mixture to the egg yolks, whisking constantly. Pour this mixture into the saucepan while stirring constantly. Return the pan to medium heat and cook, whisking constantly, until the mixture is thickened and just beginning to bubble, about 5 minutes. Remove from the heat and strain through the sieve into the bowl. Stir in the vanilla and 1 cup/115 g of the toasted coconut (reserve the remainder for topping the pies). Cover with plastic wrap, pressing the wrap directly onto the surface of the mixture, and refrigerate until well chilled, at least 3 hours or up to 3 days.

7. Just before assembling the pie, in a stand mixer fitted with the whip attachment, whip the cream until about tripled in volume. Add the remaining ¼ cup/50 g sugar and whip until soft peaks form. (Or use a large bowl and a handheld mixer or a whisk.)

8. Spoon about ¾ cup/180 ml of the coconut filling into each jar and smooth the tops. Top the filling with 2 to 3 tbsp of the whipped cream, then sprinkle the reserved toasted coconut evenly over the cream.

9. Serve immediately, or cover and refrigerate for up to 2 days, then serve chilled or at room temperature. These pies cannot be frozen.

Lemon Meringue Pie

makes 8 pies

For these pies, I like a simple lemon curd that's made in just one pan and isn't too sweet. I used to use a conventional meringue, but my old *Farm Journal* cookbook opened the door to a whole new world when I tried brown sugar meringue. Unless you're going for maximum whiteness, brown sugar meringue has a lot more texture and is more than just marshmallow-sweet like many meringues.

½ recipe Flaky Butter Crust (page 108) or 1 recipe Graham Cracker Crust (page 106)

6 tbsp/85 g unsalted butter

⅔ cup/130 g granulated sugar

½ cup/120 ml fresh lemon juice

5 eggs; 3 separated

2 tbsp grated lemon zest

3 tbsp heavy cream

Pinch of kosher salt

1 tsp vanilla extract

⅓ cup/65 g firmly packed light or dark brown sugar

1. If using the butter crust, line eight ½-pt/240-ml jars with the pastry as directed for single-crust jar pies on page 77. Refrigerate for at least 30 minutes or up to 2 days.

   Preheat the oven to 400°F/200°C/gas 6. Fit a piece of parchment paper into each pastry-lined jar, extending it beyond the rim, and fill with pie weights. Arrange the jars on a rimmed baking sheet, place in the oven, and bake for 10 minutes. Remove from the oven, lift out the weights and parchment, return the jars to the oven, and continue baking until the pastry looks dry and is golden, about 5 minutes longer. Remove from the oven and let cool completely on a baking rack before filling.

   If using the crumb crust, preheat the oven to 400°F/200°C/gas 6. Line eight ½-pt/240-ml jars with the crust and bake for 15 minutes. Remove from the oven and let cool completely on a baking rack before filling.

2. Meanwhile, place a fine-mesh sieve over a bowl. In a heavy saucepan, melt the butter over medium heat. Remove the pan from the heat and whisk in the granulated sugar, lemon juice, egg yolks, whole eggs, lemon zest, cream, and salt. Return the pan to medium-low heat and cook, stirring constantly, until the mixture has thickened, 7 to 8 minutes. Remove from the heat and strain through the sieve into the bowl. Cover with plastic wrap, pressing the wrap directly onto the surface of the mixture, and refrigerate until well chilled, at least 2 hours or up to 1 week.

CONTINUED ⟶

3. Preheat the oven to 350°F/180°C/gas 4.

4. In a stand mixer fitted with the whip attachment, whip the egg whites on medium speed until foamy. Add the vanilla, then, on low speed, gradually add the brown sugar. When all of the brown sugar has been incorporated, increase the speed to medium-high and whip until stiff, glossy peaks form. (Or, use a large bowl and a handheld mixer or a whisk.)

5. Remove the lemon curd from the refrigerator. Spoon 2 tbsp of the curd into each crust-lined jar. Top the curd with a healthy plop of meringue, using the back of a spoon to spread the meringue all the way to the edges of the jar to seal in the curd. You can make a decorative swirl or little points in the meringue, if you like.

6. Bake the pies until the meringue is just starting to brown, about 5 minutes. Remove from the oven and let cool on a baking rack until the jars feel room temperature or even cool to the touch, then serve. Or, if you like a cold lemon pie, cover and refrigerate the room-temperature pies until the jars feel cold to the touch, 1 to 2 hours, then serve. These pies will keep for up to 2 days in the refrigerator. They cannot be frozen.

Vanilla Malt Pie

makes 8 pies

COCOA PRETZEL CRUST

½ cup/115 g unsalted butter, at room temperature

1 cup/60 g coarsely crushed pretzels (from 30 pretzel sticks, 3 in/7.5 cm long)

¾ cup/75 g confectioners' sugar

⅓ cup/35 g unsweetened cocoa powder

½ cup/65 g all-purpose flour

1 egg

3 oz/85 g bittersweet chocolate, finely chopped (optional)

VANILLA MALT FILLING

3 egg yolks

2 cups/480 ml whole milk

⅔ cup/130 g granulated sugar

⅔ cup/80 g malted milk powder

¼ cup/30 g cornstarch

¼ tsp kosher salt

¼ vanilla bean

2 tbsp cold unsalted butter

This is my take on the classic Brooklyn soda fountain pairing of pretzels and a cold and creamy concoction like a chocolate egg cream or a thick malted milk. Like those drinks themselves, you can leave out the malt and opt for plain vanilla, and your pies will still be good. If you decide you don't want to cover the bottom crust with a layer of chocolate, cut the storage time by 1 day. Crush the pretzels the old-fashioned way: put them in a resealable plastic bag and pound them with a rolling pin. If you use a food processor, the crumbs will be too fine.

1. To make the crust: In a stand mixer fitted with the paddle attachment, combine the butter, ½ cup/30 g of the pretzel crumbs, and the confectioners' sugar and beat on medium-high speed until creamy. Add the cocoa powder, flour, and egg and beat just until combined. (Or, use a large bowl and a handheld mixer or a wooden spoon.) Gently fold in the remaining pretzel crumbs. The dough will be very soft. Transfer to parchment paper or plastic wrap, form into an 8-in/20-cm disk, wrap well, and refrigerate for at least 1 hour or up to 2 days.

2. On a lightly floured work surface, roll out the dough into a large square or circle about ⅛ in/3 mm thick. Cut into eight uniform squares or circles. Line eight ½-pt/240-ml jars with the dough pieces as directed for single-crust pies on page 77. Refrigerate for at least 30 minutes or up to 2 days.

3. Preheat the oven to 350°F/180°C/gas 4. Fit a piece of parchment paper into each pastry-lined jar, extending it beyond the rim, and fill with pie weights. Arrange the jars on a rimmed baking sheet, place in the oven, and bake until set and beginning to brown, about 20 minutes. Remove from the oven, lift out the weights and parchment, return the jars to the oven, and continue baking until the pastry looks dry and is browned, about 10 minutes more. Remove from the oven, transfer to a baking rack, and immediately sprinkle

with the chocolate (if using) dividing it evenly among the crusts. When the chocolate has melted, brush the chocolate to cover the bottom of each crust. Let cool completely.

4. To make the filling: In a bowl, whisk the egg yolks until blended. Set aside. Set a fine-mesh sieve over a bowl.

5. In a saucepan, combine the milk, granulated sugar, malt powder, cornstarch, and salt. Split the vanilla bean lengthwise and, using the tip of a knife, scrape the seeds into the milk mixture, then add the pod halves. Place over medium heat and cook, whisking constantly, until the mixture begins to steam and bubble at the edges of the pan, 8 to 10 minutes. Remove from the heat.

6. Gradually add about ½ cup/120 ml of the hot milk mixture to the egg yolks, whisking constantly. Pour this mixture into the saucepan while stirring constantly. Return the pan to medium heat and cook, whisking constantly, until the mixture is thickened and just beginning to bubble, about 5 minutes. Remove from the heat and whisk in the butter until melted and smooth. Strain through the sieve into the bowl. Cover with plastic wrap, pressing the wrap directly onto the surface of the mixture, and refrigerate until well chilled, at least 3 hours or up to 3 days.

7. Remove the pudding from the refrigerator and whisk or stir with a rubber spatula until smooth. Spoon about 1½ cup/120 ml of the pudding into each jar.

8. You can garnish the pies with cocoa powder, crushed pretzels, and/or sweetened whipped cream. If using the cream, in a bowl, using a whisk, whip the cream until frothy. Add the sugar and continue whipping until stiff peaks form.

9. Serve immediately, or cover and refrigerate for up to 2 days, then serve chilled or at room temperature. These pies cannot be frozen.

CHOICE OF GARNISHES

Unsweetened cocoa powder for dusting

Crushed pretzels for dusting

½ cup/120 ml chilled heavy cream

2 tsp granulated sugar

Chocolate Malt Variation

Add ⅓ cup/35 g unsweetened cocoa powder with the cornstarch and sugar, and stir in 2 oz/55 g bittersweet chocolate, finely chopped or grated, with the butter, continuing to stir until both the butter and chocolate are melted and smooth.

Peanut Butter Pie

makes 6 pies

1 recipe Graham Cracker Crust (page 106)

¾ cup/180 ml heavy cream

8 oz/225 g cream cheese, at room temperature

1 cup/280 g creamy peanut butter

⅓ cup/65 g sugar

2 tsp vanilla extract

¼ tsp kosher salt

½ cup/70 g unsalted roasted peanuts, chopped, plus more for garnish (optional)

This recipe lends itself to countless variations, especially if you, like me, enjoy peanut butter in countless variations! For example, following the directions for single-crust jar pies on page 77, line the jars with ½ recipe Flaky Butter Crust (page 108) and chill the pastry for at least 30 minutes. Then, fit a piece of parchment paper into each pastry-lined jar, fill with pie weights, arrange the jars on a rimmed baking sheet, and blind bake in a 375°F/190°C/gas 5 oven until the crust is golden, about 10 minutes. Remove the weights and parchment, spoon 2 to 3 tbsp Concord Grape Filling (page 119) into each crust, and bake until the crust is golden and dry and the grape filling bubbles, 5 to 8 minutes. Let cool completely and top with the peanut butter mousse. Or, line the jars with 1 recipe Chocolate Crumb Crust (page 107) or Cocoa Pretzel Crust (see Vanilla Malt Pie, page 86), bake as directed, then fill with the peanut butter mousse and top the filling with a thick layer of Bittersweet Ganache Filling (page 134). I thought of so many ways to dress up the peanut butter filling for these pies that I couldn't choose just one, so I opted for the easy—and always delicious—way out: plain peanut butter mousse.

1. Line six ½-pt/240-ml jars with the crust and bake as directed on page 106. Remove from the oven and let cool completely on a baking rack before filling.

2. In a stand mixer fitted with the whip attachment, whip the cream until soft peaks form. Scoop into a small bowl and reserve. (Or, use a large bowl and a handheld mixer or a whisk.)

3. Fit the stand mixer with the paddle attachment, and place the cream cheese, peanut butter, sugar, vanilla, and salt in the bowl. Beat on medium-high speed until smooth and creamy. (Or, use a large bowl and a handheld mixer or a wooden spoon.) Then, using a rubber spatula, fold in the nuts.

4. Fold about one-third of the whipped cream into the peanut butter mixture to lighten it, and then gently fold in the remaining whipped cream just until no streaks remain.

5. Spoon about ½ cup/120 ml of the filling into each jar and smooth the tops. Garnish the filling with peanuts, if desired. Cover and refrigerate for at least 1 hour or up to 3 days before serving. These pies cannot be frozen.

Chocolate Mousse Pie

makes 6 pies

I am including this pie for my brother, who requested this dessert for every family event from the time he was tiny until he entered his twenties and lost his taste for sweets (a strange, inexplicable event in our family that I feel validates my childhood taunting that he was adopted). If you like a milk chocolate mousse, substitute milk chocolate for the bittersweet.

12 oz/340 g bittersweet chocolate, chopped, or bittersweet chocolate chips (2 cups)

4 tbsp/55 g unsalted butter, cut into pieces

⅓ cup/75 ml strong brewed coffee

1 tbsp rum or Cognac

2 cups/480 ml heavy cream, chilled

1 tsp vanilla extract

½ cup/115 g Bittersweet Ganache Filling (page 134), at room temperature; 1 oz/30 g bittersweet chocolate; or 2 tbsp unsweetened cocoa

1 recipe Chocolate Crumb Crust (page 107)

1. In a large heatproof bowl or the top pan of a double boiler, combine the chocolate, butter, coffee, and rum. Set over (not touching) barely simmering water and stir constantly until melted and smooth. Remove from the heat and let cool for 15 minutes.

2. In a stand mixer fitted with the whip attachment, combine 1½ cups/360 ml of the cream and the vanilla and whip on medium-high speed until soft peaks form. (Or, use a large bowl and a handheld mixer or a whisk.)

3. Fold one-third of the whipped cream into the chocolate mixture to lighten it. Then fold in the remaining whipped cream just until combined. It's better to have some streaks of cream in your mousse then to stir the mixture until it loses its airiness. Cover the mousse and refrigerate for at least 2 hours or up to 3 days.

4. Line six ½-pt/240-ml jars with the crumb crust as directed on page 107.

5. Whip the remaining ½ cup/120 ml cream until soft peaks form. Spoon about ½ cup/120 ml mousse into each crust-lined jar. Top with about 1½ tbsp of the ganache, then top the ganache with a dollop of the whipped cream. Alternatively, top the mousse with a dollop of the cream and grate or shave a little chocolate on top or dust with cocoa powder.

6. Serve immediately, or cover and refrigerate for up to 3 days. These pies can also be frozen for up to 1 month without the cream topping. Bring to room temperature and add the cream topping just before serving.

Grasshopper Pie

makes 6 pies

2 cups/480 ml heavy
cream

1 cup/30 g loosely
packed fresh mint
leaves

1½ tsp unflavored gelatin

Ice cubes

¼ cup/50 g sugar

¼ cup/60 ml crème
de menthe

5 egg yolks

1 recipe Chocolate
Crumb Crust
(page 107)

½ cup/115 g
Bittersweet Ganache
Filling (page 134) or
2 oz/55 g bittersweet
chocolate

One word describes the grasshopper pie: *retro*. But, like many things from the 1960s, it's back—probably because chocolate and mint is an indisputable classic pairing. The cool and the rich play off each other charmingly in this bright dessert, which was probably made at a time when the crème de menthe in your liquor cabinet disappeared quickly. Now, you may move five times in a decade and lug the same bottle around (like I did). If you can't bear to bring yourself to buy a new bottle just for this recipe, you can skip it, but your filling won't be a lovely minty green and it will have a much milder mint flavor. I do not recommend using mint extract; it tastes like toothpaste. If you opt to skip steeping the fresh mint and rely on the crème de menthe alone to flavor the filling, your pies will taste more like the thin mints and Andes Candies of your childhood.

I've also seen gild-the-lily versions with crème de menthe and crème de cacao, but I reined myself in to one bottle of unused liquor here. Some people use Oreos to make the crumb crust, and marshmallows or Marshmallow Fluff in the filling.

1. In a small saucepan, combine 1½ cups/360 ml of the cream and the mint leaves and heat over medium heat until the cream begins to steam and bubble. Remove from the heat, cover, and set aside to steep for 30 minutes. Strain through a fine-mesh sieve placed over a bowl, pressing on the solids with the back of a spoon to collect as much minty cream as possible. Cover and refrigerate until using.

2. Pour the remaining ½ cup/120 ml cream into a large heatproof bowl or the top pan of a double boiler. Sprinkle the gelatin over the cream and allow the gelatin to soften for 10 minutes.

3. Meanwhile, prepare an ice bath. Use a bowl that is larger than the bowl you used for the cream and gelatin. Fill it about three-fourths full with ice cubes and water.

CONTINUED ⟶

4. Whisk the sugar, crème de menthe, and egg yolks into the cream-gelatin mixture until thoroughly combined. Set over (not touching) gently simmering water and cook, stirring constantly, until the mixture has thickened to the consistency of custard, about 10 minutes. Do not allow the mixture to boil. Remove from the heat and immediately rest the bowl in the ice bath. Continue stirring until the mixture has a puddinglike consistency, about 5 minutes.

5. In a stand mixer fitted with the whip attachment, whip the mint-infused cream on medium-high speed until soft peaks form. (Or, use a large bowl and a handheld mixer or a whisk.) Fold one-third of the whipped cream into the gelatin mixture to lighten it. Then fold in the remaining whipped cream until thoroughly combined. (This mixture can be covered and refrigerated for up to 24 hours before continuing.)

6. Line six ½-pt/240-ml jars with the crumb crust as directed on page 107.

7. Spoon about ½ cup/120 ml of the minty cream mixture into each prepared jar and smooth the tops. Garnish each pie with a spoonful of the ganache, or shave chocolate curls over the top.

8. Serve immediately, or cover and refrigerate for up to 2 days. Bring to room temperature before serving. These pies cannot be frozen.

Shepherd's Pie

makes 8 pies

To some, shepherd's pie is a nice way to use up leftovers. For others, it's an opportunity to create an ultimate comfort food à la lobster potpie or truffled macaroni and cheese. Whatever it means to you, hot, oniony meat topped with rich, cheesy mashed potatoes is a scrumptious dish. You can use lamb or beef; either one is delicious. You can also flavor the meat mixture with ½ to 1 tsp of a spice or spice mixture, such as curry powder, chili powder, ground cumin, dried oregano, or sweet or smoked paprika. The "crust" for this pie is a topping of luscious, cheesy mashed potatoes. Both the meat mixture and the potato topping can be made a day in advance. You can also reheat leftover mashed potatoes to make the topping. A final option is to mix the peas into the hot mashed potatoes instead of mixing them into the meat.

3 russet or Yukon gold potatoes (about 1¼ lb/540 g total), peeled and quartered

Kosher salt

1 tbsp olive or vegetable oil

½ cup finely chopped yellow onion

2 carrots, peeled and finely chopped

2 celery stalks, finely chopped

1 garlic clove, minced

1 lb/455 g ground beef or lamb

½ cup/120 ml beef or chicken stock

1 tbsp tomato paste

1 tbsp Worcestershire sauce

1 cup/140 g fresh or frozen green peas

Freshly ground pepper

½ cup/120 whole milk or heavy cream

½ cup/55 g grated sharp white Cheddar cheese

2 tbsp unsalted butter, at room temperature

1. In a saucepan, combine the potatoes, 1 tbsp salt, and water to cover by about 2 in/5 cm. Bring to a boil over high heat, reduce the heat to medium, and cook until the potatoes are tender when pierced with a fork, 20 to 30 minutes.

2. While the potatoes are cooking, position an oven rack in the top third of the oven and preheat the oven to 400°F/200°F/gas 6. Place eight ½-pt jars on a rimmed baking sheet.

3. In a large sauté pan, heat the olive oil over medium heat. Add the onion, carrots, and celery and cook, stirring constantly, until softened, about 5 minutes. Add the garlic and stir for 1 minute. Add the beef and cook, breaking up the meat with a wooden spoon and stirring frequently, until browned, about 10 minutes. Stir in the stock, tomato paste, and Worcestershire and cook, stirring, until the liquid has almost fully evaporated, about 3 minutes. Add the peas, stir well, and season with salt and pepper.

CONTINUED ⟶

4. When the potatoes are done, drain them. Pass them through a ricer into a bowl, or place in a bowl and beat with a handheld mixer until smooth. Add the milk, cheese, and butter and stir with a wooden spoon until smooth. Season with salt and pepper. Scoop the potato mixture into a pastry bag fitted with a large plain tip. Or, scoop the mixture into a large resealable plastic bag, and cut off one corner to make a 1-in/2.5-cm opening.

5. Divide the meat mixture among the eight jars, spooning about ⅔ cup/165 ml into each jar and packing it down gently with the back of the spoon. Each jar should be three-fourths full. Pipe about ½ cup/120 ml of the potatoes into each jar, forming a smooth, round mound on top of the meat mixture. Do not form the potato toppings into peaks, or they may singe during baking.

6. Place the jars (still on the baking sheet) on the top oven rack and bake until the potatoes begin to turn golden and the meat mixture begins to bubble, about 15 minutes. Let the pies cool for 10 minutes before serving.

The pies can cooled, covered, and refrigerated for up to 2 days. Reheat in a 350°F/180°C/gas 4 oven for 10 to 12 minutes before serving. These pies cannot be frozen.

Chicken Potpie

makes 6 pies

1 recipe Flaky Butter Crust (page 108), Luscious Lard Crust (page 110), or Versatile Cornmeal Crust (page 114)

1 tbsp olive oil

1 whole bone-in, skin-on chicken breast, about 1½ lb/680 g

2 bone-in, skin-on chicken thighs or legs, about ¾ lb/340 g

1 small yellow onion, diced

1 carrot, peeled and thinly sliced

1 celery stalk, thinly sliced

About 4 cups/900 ml chicken stock

2 tbsp unsalted butter

1 tbsp all-purpose flour

½ cup/120 ml heavy cream or sour cream

¼ cup/10 g chopped fresh flat-leaf parsley

1 cup/140 g fresh or frozen green peas

1 egg, lightly beaten, or ¼ cup/60 ml whole milk or heavy cream

These pies are the ultimate comfort food and are perfect for stashing in your freezer when you need to come up with a meal at the last minute. Plus, the recipe is flexible. You can substitute or add leeks, mushrooms, corn, parsnips, potato or sweet potato, celeriac, squash or pumpkin, or green beans to your filling, or try other herbs in place of the parsley, such as rosemary, thyme, or sage. It's your choice whether you encase your filling in pastry or only top the pie with a pastry "lid." If you opt for the lid, you'll use less dough than is called for here.

1. Following the directions in the Double-Crust Jar Pie Master Recipe (page 76), roll out the dough and cut out eight large uniform squares or circles for the bottom crusts and eight small circles for the top crusts. Line eight ½-pt jars with the bottom crusts as directed, then transfer the pastry-lined jars and the small circles to a rimmed baking sheet and refrigerate for at least 30 minutes or up to 2 days.

2. In a large, deep cast-iron frying pan or a wide, heavy saucepan, warm the olive oil over medium-high heat. Add all of the chicken and sear, turning as needed, until nicely browned on all sides, about 5 minutes per side. Transfer the chicken pieces to a plate and set aside.

3. Add the onion, carrot, and celery to the pan and cook over medium heat, stirring constantly, until softened, about 5 minutes. Return the chicken to the pan, and pour in the stock, adding enough just to cover the chicken. Cover the pan, increase the heat to medium-high, and bring to a boil. Reduce the heat to a simmer and cook until the chicken is opaque throughout, about 30 minutes.

4. Using tongs, transfer the chicken to a plate and set aside to cool. Reduce the heat under the stock mixture to low.

5. In a small frying pan, melt the butter over medium heat. Stir in the flour and cook, stirring constantly, until the mixture starts to brown and smell toasty, about 5 minutes. Stirring constantly, slowly add 1 cup/240 ml of the stock you cooked the chicken in, then continue to stir until smooth and slightly thickened, about 3 minutes. Add the cream, parsley, and peas and stir until combined. Pour the mixture into the remaining stock and mix well. Remove from the heat.

6. Pull the cooled chicken meat from the bones, discarding the bones and skin. Tear the meat into bite-size pieces. Stir the meat into the stock mixture and set aside to cool slightly.

7. Preheat the oven to 400°F/200°F/gas 6. Remove the pastry-lined jars from the refrigerator. Spoon about ⅔ cup/165 ml of the chicken mixture into each jar. You want to leave at least ¼ in/6 mm of dough above the filling uncovered so you can attach the top crust. Now, lay a dough circle on top of the filling in each jar, and use your fingers or a fork to press the edges of the crusts gently together. Cut a few small slashes in the top of each pie to allow the steam to vent. Brush pastry with beaten egg, milk, or cream.

8. Place the jars (still on the baking sheet) in the oven and bake until the top and side crusts are golden and the filling, visible through the slashes, is bubbly, about 20 minutes. Serve immediately, or let cool, cover, and refrigerate for up to 2 days, or freeze for up to 2 months. Reheat in a 350°F/180°C/gas 4 oven for about 15 minutes.

Profile: *Lasyone's Meat Pie Restaurant*

Natchitoches, Louisiana | *co-owners* Angela Lasyone and Tina Lasyone Smith

Invented in the town of Natchitoches (pronounced NACK-uh-tush), the Natchitoches pie, a flaky pastry crescent filled with an addictive mix of seasoned ground beef and pork, is so good that Louisiana has declared it an official state food. The town, which lies in the northwestern part of the state, was founded by the French in 1714 and named after the local Indian tribe. Today, it is a beautiful little spot known for its starring role in the 1989 film *Steel Magnolias* and for its friendly people, ironwork balconies, handsome river walk, and, last but not least, the annual Natchitoches Meat Pie Festival, held in September.

Meat pies are believed to date back some three hundred years in the area, to a time when the Spanish were putting down culinary roots alongside the French (the pie is reminiscent of an empanada). The delicacies evolved over the centuries, adding pork to the beef and plenty of aromatics and spices. Today, most folks agree that Lasyone's Meat Pie Restaurant makes one of the town's best versions of the famed Natchitoches meat pie. The restaurant was founded by James Lasyone, who opened it on the ground floor below the local Masons lodge in 1967. These days, the restaurant, which is in the same location—although the Masons no longer meet upstairs—is run by two sisters, Angela and Tina, daughters of James Lasyone.

Her father always loved to eat and cook, says Angela. Joking of her mother's own considerable skills at the stove, Angela says, "My dad taught her everything she knew!" But the inspiration for the restaurant came from James Lasyone's earlier career as a butcher, when he worked at the town's Live Oak Grocery. He noticed that while locals still loved their meat pies, they didn't have a place to buy them. "That's when the bright light went off," says Angela, "and he started concocting his own pies."

Despite James Lasyone's experience at the butcher counter, the success of his pies had less to do with their rich meat filling—Natchitoches pies are usually seasoned with a Creole-style mix of garlic, sweet peppers, celery, onion, and chiles—than with their crust. His pastry was a bit lighter and flakier than what enclosed other pies made at the time, explains Angela. He tasted countless pies during the years when he was a butcher, but he always found the dough too thick. "I don't know what made him come up with this dough," says Angela, "but he hit the jackpot!" If the jackpot means legions of fans, that's true.

The restaurant has appeared in the pages of *Gourmet* and *The New Yorker*, and a photograph of the facade is on the town's Wikipedia entry. In fact, a golden-brown fried meat pie at Lasyone's—about the size of a British pasty, the Natchitoches pie's kissing cousin—is not just a must-try local snack for tourists, but also something most townies stop by for. "We are definitely a meet-and-greet place," says Angela, who counts the restaurant's hospitality as just as big a draw as the dough.

Thanks in part to Angela's own cooking—she took over for her father some years ago—the place has grown into the upstairs room formerly used by the Masons. Even the take-out window had to be converted into more kitchen space to accommodate the crowds. "I told my staff," jokes

Angela, "that we were going to have to lose weight or expand. The expansion won hands down." Angela has also added a catering menu that boasts a full roster of Louisiana-style party foods, everything from filet mignon to sausage with red beans and rice to fried catfish.

Much of the restaurant's Creole-and-Cajun-accented menu, such as grits and biscuits and gravy at breakfast and shrimp po'boys and spicy fried chicken sandwiches, fried seafood platters with coleslaw and corn fritters, and even fried crawfish pies and a slew of salads the rest of the day, were added because of customer demand a few years back. "Whatever we make," says Angela of her cooking, "it is all done with a lot of good Southern flavor. There is nothing like it."

Angela helms both the restaurant and catering kitchens, while Tina arrives at 6 A.M. daily to oversee the making of hundreds of pies, which are always, always fried, says Angela. "Some people ask about baking them, but the dough reacts a little differently," she explains. "It's just not as good! Besides, in Louisiana, we boil or fry everything."

The sisters run the restaurant together full-time, splitting their duties much like their parents did throughout the early years: "Mother ran the dining rooms and the cash register and did all the book work manually," Angela recalls. "It worked good for them because she didn't tell [Dad] how to cook, and he didn't tell her how to run her dining rooms." It took the sisters a while to find their own groove, however: "When we first started working together, we were kind of like water and oil," remembers Angela. "We had different opinions and tastes on everything. But we are so much alike now that it is almost scary."

One thing they definitely share is an appreciation for their family business and for the customers who trek to Natchitoches from other states to taste their pies. "Our parents taught us fast that the only way to get ahead is hard work," says Angela, "and to remember people can always tell if you love what you are doing." That, of course, extends to the hundreds of Natchitoches meat pies that they serve each day, despite the decades that they have spent making them. "We each eat several a week," says Angela. "We are the quality control!"

LASYONE'S MEAT PIE RESTAURANT, 622 Second Street, Natchitoches, Louisiana; (318) 352-3353; www.lasyones.com

chapter four

NUTS

AND

BOLTS

✕ ✕ ✕ ✕ ✕ ✕ ✕ ✕ ✕ ✕ ✕ ✕ ✕ ✕ ✕ ✕ ✕

This chapter features recipes for the primary pie components: crusts and fillings. All of the recipes in this chapter are interchangeable: mix and match any of these crusts with any of these fillings and you'll end up with a delectable pie. Several combinations are especially brilliant, such as Blueberry Filling (page 126) with Versatile Cornmeal Crust (page 114), and Concord Grape Filling (page 119) with Luscious Lard Crust (page 110).

THE COMBOS ARE UP TO YOU.

We believe that a good crust is the key to a good pie. And we know that a good, from-scratch pie crust is not difficult to master. As with so much of cooking, especially baking, it's all about touch, and that touch is something you can learn with practice. Pie dough is primarily about the correct proportion of ingredients and how you handle the dough. Treat it lightly, and it will become flaky and tender for you.

The crusts in this chapter are interchangeable in our recipes. Find the one that works for you and use it for all your pies. Any of the doughs in this book can be frozen for up to 3 months. Tightly wrap the dough in plastic wrap, enclose it in a resealable plastic bag, and label and date the bag so you'll know what you're baking and when you made it. When it comes time to use the dough, thaw it in the refrigerator for at least 4 hours or up to overnight or at room temperature for 2 hours. If you thaw it at room temperature, refrigerate it for 15 minutes before rolling so it is not too soft.

Too often pie crusts are celebrated and fillings are relegated to the role of foil. But the quality of your filling is as important as the quality of your crust. So we've dedicated two-thirds of this chapter to the pie-making element that's easy to get right.

That's correct: fillings are easy. You can slice fresh apples, berries, peaches, pears, or apricots from the farmers' market, sprinkle them with sugar, and you've got a great pie filling. With any simple formula, of course, the outcome depends on the quality of your ingredients. Buy fresh, ripe fruit and nuts from a local farmstand or farmers' market, and use fresh spices, not the dusty nutmeg you've been carting around since college.

The fillings in this chapter are designed to work with any pie format in this book, from free-form pies to structured pies to jar pies. There are exceptions, of course, but we let you know what they are. The sweet fruit fillings are organized by season, because we believe in shopping and eating seasonally. We have also included an irresistible chocolate filling and a savory filling of greens and cheese that is perfect for both the lunch box and the hors d'oeuvre tray.

You will end up with a mess if you thaw frozen fruits for a filling. Frozen fruits release a lot of liquid when they are thawed, and this excess liquid will make your pie crust soggy and leaky. Always use the fruits frozen. It's better to let the pastry-encased fruit juices flow in a hot oven than to try to seal thawed juices into unbaked dough.

You are now ready to dive into the eighteen mix-and-match recipes in this chapter, so pick your favorites and get baking!

Two Pat-in-the-Pan Crusts: Graham Cracker and Chocolate Crumb

makes enough for six ½-pt/240 ml jars

GRAHAM CRACKER CRUST

1¼ cups/115 g graham cracker crumbs (from about 16 graham crackers, each 2 in/5 cm square)

2 tbsp sugar

5 to 6 tbsp/70 to 85 g unsalted butter, melted

Anyone can make a great pat-in-the-pan crust. The concept is simple: a yummy crisp something is crushed and moistened with melted butter. Then you press this mixture into your little cup, jar, or tin. Some crumb crusts are baked so they solidify and take on a toasty flavor; others don't need to be baked. You will find one of each kind here. You can also go wild making up your own crumb crusts. Try gingersnaps, lemon thins, shortbread, vanilla wafers, chocolate-mint thins, peanut butter cookies, HobNobs, or whatever cracker, cookie, or biscuit you like and can crush into fine crumbs. Nabisco's Famous Chocolate Wafers are the classic crushable for a chocolate crumb crust. I generally crush the cookies or crackers by pulsing them in a food processor, but you can pack them into a resealable plastic bag and crumble them finely by whacking and rolling them with a rolling pin.

GRAHAM CRACKER CRUST

1. Preheat the oven to 350°F/180°C/gas 4.

2. In a bowl, toss together the crumbs and sugar. Add the butter and stir until the mixture is evenly moist.

3. To line jars with the crust, spoon about 4 tbsp of the crumb mixture into each jar. Hold the jar in your nondominant hand (left hand if you are right-handed, for example) and start pressing the crumb mixture evenly into the bottom of the jar with your other hand. Now work some of the crumb mixture along the sides of the jar, pressing firmly. The crust should be about ¼ in/6 mm thick and cover three-fourths of the jar.

4. Transfer the lined jars to a rimmed baking sheet. Bake until lightly browned, about 15 minutes. Remove from the oven, transfer to a wire rack, and let cool completely before filling.

CHOCOLATE CRUMB CRUST

1. In a bowl, combine the crumbs and butter and stir until the mixture is evenly moist.

2. To line jars with the crust, spoon about 4 tbsp of the crumb mixture into each jar. Take the jar in your nondominant hand (left hand if you are right-handed, for example) and start pressing the crumb mixture evenly into the bottom of the jar with your other hand. Now work some of the crumb mixture along the sides of the jar, pressing firmly. The crust should be about ¼ in/6 mm thick and cover three-fourths of the jar.

3. Fill the crusts immediately.

CHOCOLATE CRUMB CRUST

1¼ cups/115 g chocolate cookie crumbs (from about 18 cookies, each 3 in/7.5 cm in diameter)

6 tbsp/85 g unsalted butter, melted

Flaky Butter Crust

makes enough for 12 to 16 free-form, structured, or jar pies

1 cup/225 g cold
unsalted butter

2 cups/255 g all-purpose
flour, plus more for
dusting

1 tsp sugar

1 tsp kosher salt

3 to 5 tbsp/45 to 75 ml
ice water

More formally known as *pâte brisée*, this workhorse crust is relatively easy to manage and bakes up wonderfully flaky. It is the ideal choice for homemade pop tarts but pairs perfectly with almost any filling in this book.

1. Cut the butter into ½-in/12-mm cubes, and freeze them while you measure and mix the dry ingredients.

2. To make the dough in a food processor: Combine the flour, sugar, and salt in the processor and pulse three or four times to mix. Retrieve the butter cubes from the freezer, scatter them over the flour mixture, and pulse until the mixture forms pea-size clumps. Add the ice water, 1 tbsp at a time, and pulse to mix, adding just enough water for the dough to come together.

   To make the dough by hand: In a large bowl, whisk together flour, sugar, and salt. Retrieve the butter cubes from the freezer and distribute them evenly in the flour mixture, coating them with the flour mixture. Sink your fingers into the mixture and begin pinching the butter and flour together, making thin, floury disks of the butter. Continue working the mixture until the butter is broken down first into floury pea-size beads and then into a loose mixture that resembles wet sand. Drizzle in 3 tbsp of the ice water and use your hand like a comb to mix in the liquid just until the dough holds together. If necessary, add additional water, 1 tbsp at a time, until the dough comes together in a crumbly mass.

   Alternatively, if using a pastry blender, whisk together the dry ingredients in a large bowl. Scatter the butter evenly over the flour mixture, and stir to coat with the flour mixture. Using a swift, downward motion, cut the butter into the dry ingredients, turning the bowl and then plunging the cutter into the mixture repeatedly. You may need to stop occasionally to slip chunks of butter from the blades back into the flour. Continue cutting until the mixture resembles wet sand. Drizzle in 3 tbsp of the water and use a fork or your fingers to mix in the liquid just until the dough holds together. If necessary, add additional water, 1 tbsp at a time, until the dough comes together in a crumbly mass.

3. Turn the dough out onto a clean, floured work surface or sheet of parchment paper. Gather the dough together in a mound, then knead it a few times to smooth it out. Divide it in half, and gently pat and press each half into a rough rectangle, circle, or square about 1 in/2.5 cm thick. The shape you choose depends on what shape you will be rolling out the dough. If you don't know how you will be using the dough at this point, opt for a circle. Wrap in plastic wrap or parchment paper and refrigerate for at least 2 hours or up to 3 days. (To freeze the dough, see page 18.)

4. To roll out, cut, shape, and fill the dough and bake the pies, see the master recipes for free-form pies, structured pies, and jar pies on pages 28, 53, and 76, respectively.

Sarah's Take on Flavored Crusts

I owe a great debt to food writer and cookbook author Melissa Clark, who wrote a piece for the *New York Times* a number of years ago in which she talked about how she tinkered around with flavored crusts for her Thanksgiving pies. Since then, I've used her insights as a springboard for my own experimenting. For example, I like to add a couple of spoonfuls of almond or hazelnut butter to a butter crust, or mix seeds from a vanilla bean into a crumb crust for a chocolate tart. Here are a few simple rules on how to flavor crusts.

You can add flavorings such as grated cheese, freshly cracked pepper, minced fresh herbs, ground nuts, or unsweetened cocoa powder—even coarsely crushed potato chips, cornflakes, or pretzels—to the dry ingredients before they are blended with the fat. You'll want to adjust the amount of seasoning based on your own taste, but as a general rule, for every 2 cups/255 g flour, you can add ¼ to ½ tsp ground spice; 2 to 4 tbsp grated cheese or minced fresh herb; or up to ½ cup/50 g cocoa powder or ground nuts.

When flavoring with a fat, you can swap out one for one, that is, 1 tbsp for 1 tbsp, but only up to a point. In the crust recipes in this book, you need to maintain at least two-thirds of the base fat for the recipe to work. Also, know that some fats are much softer than butter and will yield a crumblier dough. For good flavor without compromising structure, swap out 2 to 3 tbsp butter or lard for an equal amount of nut butter or duck, bacon, or chicken fat (schmaltz).

A note of caution: Adding textural ingredients, such as chopped or sliced nuts or coarsely shredded coconut, to the dough for small pies will make the dough more difficult to handle. They can cause tiny rips or breaches in the pastry, allowing the filling to leak out during baking or frying. These ingredients also yield a dough that is crumblier and therefore less sturdy. These textured doughs—the pretzel crust for the Vanilla Malt Pie (page 86) is a good example—are best used for jar pies.

Luscious Lard Crust

makes enough for 12 to 16 free-form, structured, or jar pies

¾ cup/170 g cold
leaf lard

2 cups/255 g
all-purpose flour,
plus more for dusting

3 tbsp sugar

½ tsp baking powder

½ tsp kosher salt

½ cup/120 ml cold
heavy cream, whole
milk, or water

My Grandpa Patrick always insisted that lard made the best pie crust, and indeed every pie crust made on the family farm in northwestern Pennsylvania was made with lard. My mother grew up with headcheese, freshly churned butter, and the annual hog-butchering season, all back-to-the-land practices that folks now pay hundreds of dollars to learn in classes. It was daily life for my Great-Grandmother Bertha, of course, who won prizes at the state fair for her famous apple pie, filled with the tart, knobby fruits from her backyard tree and capped with the flakiest of lard crusts.

This dough is softer and less crumbly to handle than the butter or cream cheese dough in this chapter, and it bakes up to a sturdy yet flaky pastry that is equally delicious with savory and sweet fillings. You can also use half lard and half unsalted butter. Finishing with cream will give you a soft, buttery dough; water will yield a slightly flakier result.

1. Cut or break the lard into 1-in/2.5-cm chunks, and freeze them while you measure and mix the dry ingredients.

2. To make the dough in a food processor: Combine the flour, sugar, baking powder, and salt in the processor and pulse three or four times to mix. Retrieve the lard chunks from the freezer, scatter them over the flour mixture, and pulse for four long bursts until the mixture resembles wet sand. Drizzle in the cream and pulse just until the dough holds together.

   To make the dough by hand: In a large bowl, whisk together the flour, sugar, baking powder, and salt. Retrieve the lard chunks from the freezer and distribute them evenly in the flour mixture, coating them with the flour mixture. Sink your fingers into the mixture and begin pinching the lard and flour together, making thin, floury disks of the lard. Continue working the mixture until the lard is broken down first into floury pea-size beads and then into a loose mixture that resembles wet sand. Drizzle in the cream and use your hand like a comb to mix in the liquid just until the dough holds together.

Alternatively, if using a pastry blender, whisk together the dry ingredients in a large bowl. Scatter the lard evenly over the flour mixture, and stir to coat with the flour mixture. Using a swift, downward motion, cut the lard into the dry ingredients, turning the bowl and then plunging the cutter into the mixture repeatedly. You may need to stop occasionally to slip chunks of lard from the blades back into the flour. Continue cutting until the mixture resembles wet sand. Drizzle in the cream and use a fork or your fingers to mix in the liquid just until the dough holds together.

3. Turn the dough out onto a clean, floured work surface or a sheet of parchment paper. Gather the dough together in a mound, then knead it a few times to smooth it out. Divide it in half, and gently pat and press each half into a rough rectangle, circle, or square about 1 in/2.5 cm thick. The shape you choose depends on what shape you will be rolling out the dough. If you don't know how you will be using the dough at this point, opt for a circle. Wrap in plastic wrap or parchment paper and refrigerate for at least 30 minutes or up to 3 days. (To freeze the dough, see page 18.)

4. To roll out, cut, shape, and fill the dough and bake the pies, see the master recipes for free-form pies, structured pies, and jar pies on pages 28, 53, and 76, respectively.

Profile: *The Original Fried Pie Shop*

Davis, Oklahoma | *owner and founder* Nancy Fulton

From her first day in business, Nancy Fulton wanted to make sure anybody driving past Exit 51 on I-35 in Davis, Oklahoma, would know what she was selling. So without much money for signage, she improvised: "We painted FRIED PIES in big, red block letters on the side of a large, white building," she laughs, "and nothing else."

The giant words worked. On that first morning, outfitted with nothing but a FryDaddy, Nancy started cooking. Her original plan had been to stack up a batch of her freshly fried pies—thick-crusted, fat beauties made with locally milled flour and stuffed with sweet, sweet peach or blackberry filling—as a display to lure potential customers. But the folks streamed in, and the pies left with them. She sold so many so fast, Nancy recalls, that the fancy display never happened. "I tell people that once they stop, they're our customers."

She's right. These days Nancy is an Oklahoma legend, her original location sells three thousand pies a day in the summer. And thanks to the addition of two big, fire-engine-red FRIED PIES signs north and south of Exit 51, legions of hungry travelers making the long trek from Canada to Mexico on I-35 routinely build in a stop at Nancy's. Of course, the little shop, in an old filling station at the foot of the beautiful Arbuckle Mountains, is worth a trip all by itself. It's still fitted with a working pump, a 1960s Sinclair Gas dinosaur, and a beautiful no-name rooster who "begs like a dog for pies," laughs Nancy. As pretty as he is, she says, he rarely gets them.

Demand is so high for her fried handiwork that Nancy has expanded to multiple Original Fried Pie Shops in three states (Oklahoma, Texas, and Arkansas), and she has franchised her Arbuckle Mountains pie business to those willing to follow her strict guidelines, which include pies made by hand daily from fresh dough that calls for a dry mix she jokingly calls "Nancyquick." Now, a half dozen places make her fried pies in several states, among them The Fried Pie Wagon in Decatur, Texas; Grandma Paddles in Princeton, Illinois; and even an outpost called Mimi's in the tony Colorado ski resort town of Breckenridge, where the owner had to tweak the recipe for high altitudes.

Fried pies are ubiquitous in Texas and Oklahoma, but Nancy's are held in particularly high regard. She attributes their reputation to three things. One is the secret method she uses for mixing the dough. Two is a strict approach to the core yin and yang of the dessert: her fruit, nut, and cream fillings—there are now twenty-eight flavors total, including a few meat pies and a bacon and eggs pie for breakfast—are thick and very sweet, while the dough itself is sugar free.

And three is that with the exception of a machine roller for thinning the dough and a special crimper she designed to help make short work of creating the "fork prints" on her pies' puffy edges, everything is done by hand. "I squeeze in lemon juice, just like I would if I were making it at home," she says. The main difference, of course, is that she is now squeezing juice from a bushel of lemons.

Nancy uses fresh fruits and peanut oil, and she uses local products whenever she can, including butter from a nearby dairy and flour from the Shawnee Milling Company, which sits just about an hour and a half north of the shop. She insists that Shawnee flour provides a flavor that she has never been able to replicate with any nationally sold brand. "I really think it's the best," she says. In fact, Nancy's fried pies earned the state "Made in Oklahoma" seal of approval because of their percentage of locally produced products.

"That is the thing that I've got going for me that many other businesses don't have," says Nancy of her commitment to using the same ingredients and methods throughout her career, instead of tinkering to make her business more cost-effective. "I could add water to my fruit and make a lot more money . . . but maybe not, because my customers wouldn't come back," she muses. "I would have to go back to doing things the old-fashioned way."

In fact, Nancy has never stopped doing things the old-fashioned way. Her recipe is more than one hundred years old, passed down by her mother, Louise Knutson, from *her* mother, Nancy Posey. (With any luck, Nancy's grandson Beaux, named after her husband, will one day carry the skill with sweets to a fifth generation. He's just getting ready to graduate from college, she says, "and he can make a good fried pie.") Nancy Posey started the family business in 1893, selling her pies to the Oklahoma cowboys working the cattle ranches that sprawled at the base of the Arbuckle Mountains. According to family legend, it was a bitter winter, and the cowboys had to cook their dinners over an open campfire. Fried pies were easy to heat in the flames and provided a bit of sweet respite in the cold. Nancy made them from local apples and peaches she dried herself and from Arbuckle Mountains water, which locals claim is some of the purest in the world. They were fried in lard and carried through the hills in old metal buckets that once captured maple syrup.

Today's Nancy started her own business in scarce times, too. It was 1993, she was unemployed, and her husband, Beaux, had become disabled, losing the use of both of his legs. "I'd been to job interview after job interview," she recalls, but wasn't making any progress. She and Beaux had once run a full-service restaurant, so they knew they could open a small business that served food. But they also knew that a food business is hard work, and that whatever they decided to do, it had to be something, jokes Nancy, that they could run "with only two legs between us." It had to be simple, and it had to have crystal-clear focus, Nancy recalls thinking. And "we had to do it so well that people would come back."

These days, Nancy insists that the business is successful in part because of her customers' memories: fried pies were made not just by Nancy's grandmother, but by grandmothers all over Oklahoma. "When folks open our front door they're thinking about someone they love who used to make them fried pies, and they loved them and maybe they're not around anymore," says Nancy. "That's half the battle right there." And judging from the steady stream of people who travel up I-35 to the Arbuckle Mountains for one of Nancy's original fried pies, it's a battle she's winning.

THE ORIGINAL FRIED PIE SHOP, *U.S. 77 and I-35, Davis, Oklahoma; (580) 369-7830; www.theoriginalfriedpieshop.com*

Versatile Cornmeal Crust

makes enough for 12 to 16 free-form, structured, or jar pies

¾ cup/170 g cold
unsalted butter

1½ cups/195 g
all-purpose flour,
plus more for dusting

½ cup/70 g cornmeal

½ cup/100 g sugar

1 tsp kosher salt

2 egg yolks

2 to 3 tbsp ice water

Cornmeal crust is the perfect foil for meaty and cheesy savory pies—and for blueberries! There's something charmed about the combination of cornmeal and blueberries: the tartness, the corny flavor, and the toothsome texture live in perfect harmony.

This is a crumbly dough, which means that free-form pies with juicy fillings larger than 4 in/10 cm square or round are hard to handle when baked. A 4-in/10-cm pie is the sweet spot. Because it is crumbly, it is also a great pat-in-the-pan dough for structured pies. You can use yellow, white, or blue cornmeal, though yellow makes the most attractive pies.

1. Cut the butter into ½-in/12-mm cubes, and freeze them while you measure and mix the dry ingredients.

2. To make the dough in a food processor: Combine the flour, cornmeal, sugar, and salt in the processor and pulse three or four times to mix. Retrieve the butter cubes from the freezer, scatter them over the flour mixture, and pulse until the mixture forms pea-size clumps. In a small bowl, whisk together the egg yolks and 2 tbsp of the ice water. Drizzle the yolk mixture into the flour mixture and pulse just until the dough holds together. If the dough does not come together, pulse in the remaining 1 tbsp ice water.

To the make the dough by hand: In a large bowl, whisk together flour, cornmeal, sugar, and salt. Retrieve the butter cubes from the freezer and distribute them evenly in the flour mixture, coating them with flour mixture. Sink your fingers into the mixture and begin pinching the butter and flour together, making thin, floury disks of the butter. Continue working the mixture until the butter is broken down first into floury pea-sized beads and then into a loose mixture that resembles wet sand. In a small bowl, whisk together the egg yolks and 2 tbsp of the ice water. Drizzle the yolk mixture into the flour mixture and use your hand like a comb to mix in the liquid just until the dough holds together. If necessary, work in the remaining 1 tbsp ice water until the dough comes together in a crumbly mass.

Alternatively, if using a pastry blender, whisk together the dry ingredients in a large bowl. Scatter the butter evenly over the flour mixture, and stir to coat with the flour mixture. Using a swift, downward motion, cut the butter into the dry ingredients, turning the bowl and then plunging the cutter into the mixture repeatedly. You may need to stop occasionally to slip chunks of butter from the blades back into the flour. Continue cutting until the mixture resembles wet sand. In a small bowl, whisk together the egg yolks and 2 tbsp of the ice water. Drizzle the yolk mixture into the flour mixture and use a fork or your fingers to mix in the liquid just until the dough holds together. If necessary, work in the remaining 1 tbsp ice water until the dough comes together in a crumbly mass.

3. Turn the dough out onto a clean, floured work surface or sheet of parchment paper. Gather the dough together in a mound, then knead it a few times to smooth it out. Divide it in half and gently pat and press each half into a rough rectangle, circle, or square about 1 in/2.5 cm thick. The shape you choose depends on what shape you will be rolling out the dough. If you don't know how you will be using the dough at this point, opt for a circle. Wrap in plastic wrap or parchment paper and refrigerate for at least 2 hours or up to 2 days. (To freeze the dough, see page 18.)

4. To roll out, cut, shape, and fill the dough and bake the pies, see the master recipes for free-form pies, structured pies, and jar pies on pages 28, 53, and 76, respectively.

Sturdy Cream Cheese Crust

makes enough for 12 to 16 free-form, structured, or jar pies

Cream cheese dough is a winner with handheld pies. It's crumbly and yet strong enough to be manhandled and munched and travels beautifully. It warmly welcomes savory additions, such as herbs and cracked black pepper, and is equally great with sweet fillings, because the cream cheese imparts a gentle tang. If you want your pies to bake up gorgeously golden, brush the dough with egg wash or cream before putting in the oven.

4 tbsp/55 g cold
   unsalted butter

4 oz/115 g cold
   cream cheese

2 cups/255 g
   all-purpose flour,
   plus more for dusting

1 tbsp sugar

1 tsp kosher salt

¼ cup/60 ml cold
   whole milk, plus
   2 tbsp if needed

1. Cut the butter into ½-in/12-mm cubes and the cream cheese into 1-in/2.5-cm cubes, and freeze them while you measure and mix the dry ingredients.

2. To make the dough in a food processor: Combine the flour, sugar, and salt in the processor and pulse three or four times to mix. Retrieve the butter and cream cheese cubes from the freezer, scatter them over the flour mixture, and pulse until the mixture forms pea-size clumps. Add the ¼ cup/60 ml milk and pulse three or four times until the dough comes together. If it does not come together, add the additional 2 tbsp milk, 1 tbsp at a time, pulsing after each addition.

To make the dough by hand: In a large bowl, whisk together the flour, sugar, and salt. Retrieve the butter and cream cheese cubes from the freezer and distribute them evenly in the flour mixture, coating them with the flour mixture. Sink your fingers into the mixture and begin pinching the fats and flour together, making thin, floury disks of the butter and cream cheese cubes. Continue working the mixture until the fats are broken down first into floury pea-size beads and then into a loose mixture that resembles wet sand. Drizzle in the ¼ cup/60 ml milk and use your hand like a comb to mix in the liquid just until the dough holds together. If necessary, add the additional 2 tbsp milk, 1 tbsp at a time, until the dough comes together in a crumbly mass.

Alternatively, if using a pastry blender, whisk together the dry ingredients in a large bowl. Scatter the butter and cream cheese cubes evenly over the flour mixture, and stir to coat with the flour mixture. Using a swift,

CONTINUED ⟶

downward motion, cut the fats into the dry ingredients, turning the bowl and then plunging the cutter into the mixture repeatedly. You may need to stop occasionally to slip chunks of fat from the blades back into the flour. Continue cutting until the mixture resembles wet sand. Drizzle in the ¼ cup/60 ml milk and use a fork or your fingers to mix in the liquid just until the dough holds together. If necessary, add additional milk, 1 tbsp at a time, until the dough comes together in a crumbly mass.

3. Turn the dough out onto a clean, floured work surface or a sheet of parchment paper. Gather the dough together in a mound, then knead it a few times to smooth it out. Divide it in half, and gently pat and press each half into a rough rectangle, circle, or square about 1 in/2.5 cm thick. The shape you choose depends on what shape you will be rolling out the dough. If you don't know how you will be using the dough at this point, opt for a circle. Wrap in plastic wrap or parchment paper and refrigerate for at least 2 hours or up to 3 days. (To freeze the dough, see page 18.)

4. To roll out, cut, shape, and fill the dough and bake the pies, see the master recipes for free-form pies, structured pies, and jar pies on pages 28, 53, and 76, respectively.

Concord Grape Filling

makes enough for 24 to 32 free-form or structured pies or 12 jar pies

If you are driven by nostalgia to capture the flavor of Welch's grape jelly, you are in for quite a bit of work, thanks to the seeds and the intensely colored flesh of Concord grapes. But all that labor is totally worth it. Wear a dark color and be prepared to sport stained fingernails for a few days—a badge of honor for deliciousness. Gloves are not a solution. Skinning a grape with gloved hands is a very slippery task.

This recipe makes far more grape filling than you'll need for one batch of handheld pies, but scaling the recipe down results in a less tasty filling. If you're not planning on a grape-pie frenzy, you can freeze the filling. It keeps beautifully for several months. One recipe will fill two batches of handheld pies or one 9-in/23-cm pie.

And, yes, Concord grapes, with their tart yet musky flavor, are irreplaceable in this recipe. I tested other grape varieties and never found a winner.

2 lb/910 g Concord grapes (about 8 cups), stemmed

½ cup/100 g sugar

4 tsp cornstarch

1. Working over a large bowl, pinch each grape so the pulp slips from the loose skin. The pulp and seeds will slip right out, along with some juice, which you'll also want to catch in the bowl. (That's why Concords, along with green, sweet southern Scuppernongs, are known as slip-skin grapes.) Do not discard the skins. Instead, reserve them in a large heatproof bowl.

2. Transfer the pulp and juice to a large saucepan. Place over medium-high heat and bring to a boil. Cook until the seeds separate from the pulp and the pulp loses its shape, 10 to 12 minutes. The mixture will bubble furiously. Stir frequently to prevent scorching. When the seeds begin to float to the top, remove the pan from the heat.

3. Pour the hot grape pulp through a fine-mesh sieve into the bowl holding the grape skins, pressing on the solids to push as much pulp through as possible. Mix together the strained pulp and skins.

4. In a small bowl, stir together the sugar and cornstarch. Add to the hot pulp and skin mixture and stir to mix. Let cool to room temperature, then cover tightly and refrigerate for at least 2 hours or up to 2 days. Use immediately, or freeze for up to 4 months.

Cherry Filling

makes enough for 12 to 16 free-form or structured pies or 6 jar pies

3½ to 4 cups/800 to 910 g pitted and halved fresh or frozen sour cherries (if frozen, do not thaw)

¾ cup/150 g sugar

1 tbsp fresh lemon juice

2 tbsp cornstarch

½ tsp vanilla extract

¼ tsp salt

Cherry is my dad's favorite pie flavor, and in Pennsylvania, where I grew up, cherry season passes in the blink of an eye. It wasn't until I moved to California that I experienced a slightly longer season, but I still had a hard time getting my hands on the sour cherries I believe are necessary for a proper cherry pie filling. Sour cherries, also known as pie cherries or tart cherries, are harvested in late spring or early summer, and Montmorency, Morello, and Early Richmond are the best-known varieties. You can make a pie with sweet cherries, such as Bing or Rainier, though I much prefer the tartness of their sour cousins. If you're using sweet cherries, cut the sugar in half and add 1 to 2 tbsp fresh lemon juice.

In a bowl, combine all of the ingredients and mix gently so as not to crush the cherries. Use immediately.

Raspberry-Rhubarb Filling

makes enough for 12 to 16 free-form or structured pies or 6 jar pies

1 cup/140 g thinly sliced rhubarb

1 cup/115 g fresh or frozen raspberries (if frozen, do not thaw)

⅓ cup/65 g firmly packed light brown sugar

1 tbsp cornstarch

½ tsp kosher salt

Rhubarb has two seasons: one in early spring and one in late fall. And, yes, I know strawberry and rhubarb is the classic pie combo. But part of me can't get over how disappointed I was when I bit into my first piece of supersweet strawberry-rhubarb pie, only to discover that it wasn't just strawberry. The other part of me simply loves raspberries much more than strawberries. The combination of raspberry and rhubarb makes a tarter filling, and when the pie is broken open, a gorgeous fuchsia hue is revealed. If you can't break from the traditional strawberry-rhubarb combination, substitute 1½ cups/170 g strawberries for the raspberries and add 1 tsp fresh lemon juice

In a bowl, combine all of the ingredients and mix gently so as not to crush the berries. Use immediately.

Profile: *Grand Traverse Pie Company*

Traverse City, Michigan | *co-owners* Mike and Denise Busley

The story of the Grand Traverse Pie Company—the chain's headquarters are way up north, in the heart of Michigan's Montmorency cherry orchards—actually begins near the Southern California coast, in the small apple-growing town of Julien. It's located halfway between Palm Springs and San Diego, where Mike and Denise Busley were living in 1994. Like many couples, they were juggling two small children and two successful but stressful careers: Denise was in the competitive world of medical sales, and Mike was an executive working for an aerospace engineering company in the process of shrinking its business footprint. "Part of my job was notifying people that they had to leave," he wryly recalls. "It wasn't much fun."

Despite holding secure jobs with good salaries, Mike and Denise longed to return to their roots in southern Michigan (or Downstate, to natives). "We wanted a simpler life," said Mike. "We wanted to control our destinies."

One day, on a road trip, they stumbled into the tiny Julien Pie Shop, run by Liz Smothers with help from sons David, Tim, and Dan, who tends the family apple orchards. After the Busleys left, they couldn't shake the taste and smell of the wonderful pies. More important, they couldn't get over the congeniality of the people who were baking them. They left not only with full bellies, but also with an idea for a business. "Maybe we can make pies," Mike remembers saying later to Denise, "back in Traverse City?"

In retrospect, it was a ridiculous notion. "I think Denise had made only one pie in her life before that visit," Mike jokes. They had never run their own small business, either. And they weren't even from Traverse City, which is so far north in Michigan that most Downstaters consider it to be another state. But Mike was experienced in business strategy, and he took his research seriously. Just as Julien was in the heart of Southern California apple country and near a big state park, Traverse City had both a famous local crop, cherries, and a major tourist draw, Lake Michigan. "Most people don't know it," Mike says, "but 70 percent of the nation's tart cherries come from around Traverse City. It is truly cherry country." In fact, every Fourth of July, half a million people stream into the area for the annual festival celebrating the tart Montmorency cherry—the cherry that any baker will tell you is the only cherry that should be in a pie.

Not surprisingly, cherry pies are a big deal in Traverse City, sought out by locals and visitors alike. But back in 1994, when Mike and Denise first began thinking about making pies there, there wasn't a sit-down-and-enjoy-a-slice-and-a-cup-of-coffee-and-the-paper kind of pie shop in town. Their idea seemed promising. For a year, Mike worked on his business plan. "It was," he admits, "my therapy for a while." He defined the competition, studied the town's economic landscape, and figured out what it would cost to run the place. "But I knew my limitations," says Mike. He and Denise still didn't know how to make pies. So he decided to call Liz Smothers and ask her if she would review his proposal for a family-style pie shop.

Smothers could have turned him away for any number of reasons, recalls Mike, but instead she read the plan carefully. Then, drawing on her more than sixty years of experience in the pie business, she went even further, filling in lots of practical information that Mike and Denise could not have known: the cost of ingredients, the amount of kitchen space required, equipment and storage needs, daily work flow—all the details you would never know without years of daily pie baking. "Liz has an industrial engineering mind," Mike says admiringly, "even though every step—rolling crusts, peeling apples—is done by hand."

Liz was more than a savvy businesswoman, however. She was also a great pie baker, and luckily for Mike and Denise, she was willing to share what she knew. To do that, she insisted the couple go to work for her, at least for a few days: "We threw on aprons and got to work making pies," Mike remembers, "and despite my achy knees, I loved it. You could see the results of your work every day—not just the pies themselves but also the smiles of the customers who bought them."

With the help of three Julien pies they brought with them to the meeting, Mike and Denise secured a small-business loan from a Michigan bank and then opened their Grand Traverse Pie Company in 1996. Liz came on as a consultant to help them with the recipes for the dough for their whole pies—"We haven't changed that one bit in fourteen years," says Mike—and their hand pies. The latter they call turnovers and describe as "a little piece of heaven wrapped in our golden, flaky pie crust." Liz also helped them develop their fillings, the peach, plum, blueberry, and, the most critical of all, tart cherry. That last one has seven variations,

including the cherry crumb, which was called "a religious experience" by celebrity chef Mario Batali, who summers in Michigan. Although most filling recipes also stay the same, that cherry must be adjusted each June, says Mike, because yearly differences in rain and sun levels affect the sugar and moisture content of the local fruits.

From the day the shop opened, Mike and Denise have been on the front lines, doing everything from rolling out the dough and cooking down the cherries and berries to greeting the customers and sweeping the floors. Now, nearly fifteen years later, there are more than a dozen Grand Traverse pie shops in two states, all of them community-minded operations selling pies made from scratch. "We wanted the simpler life, wanted to run a business that felt like a family, that was a family," says Mike, recalling the dream that he and Denise shared over that first piece of Liz Smothers's apple pie in 1994. And so they have, literally: their daughter, Kellee, and son, Bobby, both college graduates, now help bake and sell pies at the second Traverse City shop, a place they helped build from the ground up.

GRAND TRAVERSE PIE COMPANY
525 West Front Street, Traverse City, Michigan;
(231) 922-7437; www.gtpie.com

Raspberry (or Other Tart Berry) Filling

makes enough for 12 to 16 free-form or structured pies or 6 jar pies

There's a gorgeous world of berries out there, and many are regional. On a cross-country camping trip I took when I was twenty, I ordered pie in almost every state of the union. In Utah, it was blackberry pie; in coastal California, it was marionberries; and in Washington, olallieberries. In my home state of Pennsylvania, elderberries, mulberries, red and golden currants, and fat blackberries would appear at the farmers' market in late summer. (For these tart berries, you need to ramp up the sugar in this recipe.) But raspberries seem to be everywhere, so they set the template for using other berries for pies.

2 cups/225 g fresh or frozen raspberries (if frozen, do not thaw)

¼ to ½ cup/40 to 90 g loosely packed light or dark brown or granulated sugar

1 tbsp all-purpose flour

½ tsp grated lemon zest

Pinch of kosher salt

In a bowl, combine all of the ingredients, adding the sugar to taste. Mix gently so as not to crush the berries. Use immediately.

Blueberry Filling

makes enough for 12 to 16 free-form or structured pies or 6 jar pies

3 cups/340 g fresh or frozen blueberries (if frozen, do not thaw)

¼ cup/50 g sugar

1½ tbsp cornstarch

1 tsp fresh lemon juice

1 tsp grated lemon zest

Pinch of freshly grated nutmeg (optional)

Use this filling with a schmear of mascarpone cheese when making handheld pies for your next picnic. If you use frozen blueberries, look for tiny, tart wild blueberries. Or, better yet, buy blueberries in bulk at the farmers' market at the height of the season and freeze them yourself, for use when the days turn cool. You can also add 1 or 2 tbsp of maple syrup to this filling and use it to make pop tarts. (Follow the directions for Peanut Butter and Jelly Pop Tarts on page 32, substituting 1 tbsp plus 2 tsp of the blueberry mixture for the filling.)

In a bowl, combine all of the ingredients and mix gently so as not to crush the berries. Use immediately.

Apricot or Peach Filling

makes enough for 12 to 16 free-form or structured pies or 6 jar pies

Apricots are such a gorgeous fruit, with such a fleeting season, that I like to capture their essence in the simplest way possible: barely sweetened, with a touch of lemon juice for tang. Peach season is longer, and a highlight of the summer, but I celebrate peaches simply as well. If you want to dress up the filling, you can add a little ground ginger or freshly grated nutmeg. Apricots and peaches are also delicious paired with almonds, so a little splash of almond extract or ½ cup/70 g toasted slivered blanched almonds would be a good addition to this filling. If you crave this pie outside of apricot or peach season, Willamette Valley Fruit Company offers flavorful frozen fruit (see Sources, page 139). These same proportions work with fresh plums: I leave the skins on for their gorgeous color and a little pucker.

3 cups/500 g thinly sliced fresh or frozen apricots or peaches (if frozen, do not thaw)

½ cup/100 g sugar

2 tbsp cornstarch

1 tsp fresh lemon juice

Pinch of kosher salt

In a bowl, combine all of the ingredients and mix gently so as not to crush the fruit. Use immediately.

Apple Filling

makes enough for 12 to 16 free-form or structured pies or 6 jar pies

4 cups/680 g peeled and thinly sliced or diced apples (3 large apples)

⅔ cup/130 g firmly packed light or dark brown sugar

1 tbsp all-purpose flour

1 tsp fresh lemon juice

½ to 1 tsp ground cinnamon

⅛ to ¼ tsp ground ginger

Pinch of kosher salt

When it comes to baking, not all apples are created equal. The expansion of farmers' markets throughout the United States and the United Kingdom has introduced many delectable varieties with tastes and textures that are ideal for baking. Cortland, Idared, Winesap, and Honeycrisp (even the name is delicious) are just a few of the varieties I now see. Supermarkets carry a wider selection of apples these days, too.

I like to combine a couple of varieties (Idared and Northern Spy is my favorite pairing), and I often include a Granny Smith for its puckery, crisp flesh. When in doubt, ask the farmer what works best for pie—or know that you can't go wrong with a mixture of readily available Granny Smith and McIntosh apples.

In a bowl, combine all of the ingredients. Let stand until the apples give up some of their juices, 15 to 30 minutes. Use immediately.

Quince Variation

If I see quinces at the market, I always buy a couple. They turn this filling slightly pink and add an intoxicating fragrance and lots of flavor. Replace ½ to 1 cup/85 to 170 g of the sliced apples with an equal amount of diced or shredded quince. Because quinces are not as sweet as apples, you may want to adjust the sugar, too, adding another 1 to 3 tbsp. If you can't find fresh quinces, which are still sold seasonally, capture their lovely autumnal flavor by dicing 3 to 4 tbsp prepared quince paste and stirring it into the apple mixture.

Dried Apple and Raisin Filling

makes enough for 12 to 16 free-form or structured pies or 6 jar pies

This classic Southern fried-pie filling will perfume your kitchen with a spicy, autumnal fragrance. Other dried fruits can be substituted for the raisins; cranberries or cherries are especially nice because of their tartness. If you are baking free-form pies rather than frying them, add a sliver of butter to the filling in each one for a hint of richness. If you are baking structured pies, you can also add a little of the strained cider liquid to the filling for extra flavor. Dilute the remaining strained cider with some sparkling water or seltzer and enjoy the apple spritzer with your pie.

3 cups/270 g dried apples

3 cups/720 ml apple cider

½ cup/85 g dark raisins or golden raisins

3 tbsp firmly packed light or dark brown sugar

2 tbsp cornstarch

1 tsp ground cinnamon

¼ tsp ground ginger

¼ tsp freshly grated nutmeg

Pinch of kosher salt

1. In a large saucepan, combine the apples and cider over medium heat, bring to a simmer, and simmer, uncovered, until the apples have softened, about 20 minutes. Remove from the heat, stir in the raisins, and let cool for 30 minutes.

2. Pour the mixture through a sieve placed over a measuring pitcher or bowl. Reserve the liquid for flavoring a filling for structured pies or for mixing up a spritzer (see headnote). In a bowl, combine the drained apples and raisins, the sugar, cornstarch, spices, and salt and mix well.

3. Use immediately, or cover and refrigerate for up to 3 days.

Profile: *Hubig's Pies*

New Orleans, Louisiana | *co-owner* Drew Ramsey

Plenty of dishes are at home in the great food city of New Orleans: a po'boy piled high with cornmeal-crusted oysters, Creole tomatoes, and shredded lettuce; a big bowl of red beans and rice doused with Crystal hot sauce; a pot of gumbo brimming with sweet Gulf shrimp and heady with spices. But natives would no doubt add another item to that list: a Hubig's fried hand pie, its glassine bag decorated with a cartoon image of a full-bellied baker, wearing a floppy chef's hat emblazoned with the words *Savory Simon*, twirling a steaming-hot pie.

In New Orleans, forget Hostess. Hubig's pies, made in simple flavors like lemon, sweet potato, apple, peach, chocolate, coconut, and blueberry, are the sweet snack sold in every corner store in the city for a buck and change. They have been made in the same low-slung white building in the Faubourg Marigny district, just east of the French Quarter, since 1922, and the dough is still made with lard. Old-fashioned cooks know that's what yields great flavor.

And that chubby cook who has been depicted on every package for just as long is Simon Hubig, who founded the company in Fort Worth, Texas, near the start of World War I. Hubig was an immigrant—he had roots in Germany and in the Basque region where Spain meets France, and when he arrived in the States, he took a job as a baker (his mother had been one in Europe) in his new home.

Simon Hubig's pies were good, but his business skills were better, insists Andrew Ramsey, the third generation of his family to help run Hubig's in New Orleans. "He was somewhat of a visionary," says Andrew, known by friends as Drew, "a franchiser before the word was even in the English language."

At one time, Simon Hubig owned dozens of satellite bakeries and distribution centers in the Southeast and along the East Coast, traveling by train to check on his empire, which included a few minor-league sports teams in addition to pies. "He was an entrepreneur," says Drew, "by every definition of the word."

As it turns out, Drew's grandfather Otto was also a keen businessman. He arrived in New Orleans from Texas with an MBA to help run the shop, eventually buying a stake in it in 1950. (In the 1970s, Otto Jr., Drew's dad, brought in another partner, Lamar Bowman.) Otto Sr. was such a good manager that after the Depression and World War II took their toll on Hubig's—during the war, the flour and sugar needed to make pies were rationed, as were the rubber and petroleum needed to deliver them—the New Orleans branch was the only one left standing. In retrospect, it might have been the company's treatment of its bakers rather than its bottom line that saved the franchise: staffers donated their own ration stamps to help the company make its pies.

The employees were saviors more recently, too, in the months after Hurricane Katrina in 2005, when the storm destroyed the company along with much of the city. Hubig's delivery trucks were buried deep under mud, and its employees, most now homeless, had evacuated across the South. But the company decided not only to issue paychecks from its rainy-day fund, but also to provide transportation back to New Orleans: "We sent bus tickets to the Red Cross in Atlanta, to government refugee camps in western Louisiana," says Drew. "We sent bus tickets to churches. We had to get our workers back." Not surprisingly, the company eventually went bankrupt trying to save itself.

It is not what most businessmen would have done, and if you ask Drew why he chose that path, he's slow to respond. "It was the right thing to do," he says, choking up a bit. "It needed to be done." It worked, too. The employees came back, coming in unpaid until the company began to earn money. The people who sold him his sugar and flour gave him supplies on credit; so did the auto shop that maintained his delivery trucks. And although today the trucks do far fewer routes than they once did, Hubig's is now back up to making twenty-five to thirty thousand pies a day—a number that would have made old Simon Hubig proud.

Drew returned the favor, delivering pies in those first post-Katrina weeks to anyone who asked for them—even to corner stores that were now nothing more than a concrete slab. "I'm not going to say no to somebody with a plastic tarp and an Igloo ice chest where his shop used to be," says Drew. "That's a store Hubig's had served for seventy-five years: my grandfather dealt with somebody else's grandfather, my dad dealt with somebody else's dad. We buy locally whenever possible."

It's an old-fashioned idea that meshes with the current passion for locally sourced, seasonal food, a sentiment that has never left food-focused New Orleans. With the exception of the banana and lemon pies, most of the fruits in Hubig's preservative-free sweets come from Louisiana, as does the sugar. "We don't open up a can of pie filling," says Drew. "The farmer harvests 'em and we clean and boil 'em and make sweet potato pie."

And not every kind of pie is available all year, either. For example, Hubig's fans know that peach comes in summer and sweet potato in fall, and whole pies, which decades ago were Hubig's main draw, are now made for holidays only. "When was the last time you got together as a family for a meal?" says Drew of Hubig's decision to focus on pocket pies. Sales of the whole pies were dropping, he recalls, "while the little glazed pie was heading north."

Even if you don't sit down to dinner, Drew says you should always take the time to heat up your hand pie, as suggested on the package. "And you should also put a scoop of vanilla ice cream between the two halves," he adds, "trust me."

The loss of whole pies and the addition of a banana filling about fifteen years ago are among the few things that Hubig's has changed with the times. (Okay, they did add T-shirts post-Katrina and put "Hu-Dat?!" on their bags after the Saints won the Super Bowl.) "We don't subscribe to the church of what's happening now," says Drew. "Can't you do diabetic friendly? Yeah, I probably could, but I'm not." In fact, even the metal die that cuts out their 4-oz/115-g pies hasn't changed a bit in nearly eighty years. Not that those who remember their first bite of a Hubig's fried pie before World War II would believe him. "You meet old-timers," jokes Drew, "who insist they used to be bigger."

HUBIG'S PIES, 2417 Dauphine Street, New Orleans, Louisiana; (800) 232-0269; www.hubigs.com

Pear-Ginger Filling

makes enough for 12 to 16 free-form or structured pies or 6 jar pies

2 cups/300 g diced pears (about 3 large pears, in ½-in/12-mm dice)

¼ cup/50 g firmly packed light brown sugar

1 tbsp all-purpose flour

⅛ to ¼ tsp ground ginger

Pinch of kosher salt

I cannot eat a raw pear without developing a terrible stomachache! But I love pears in every other form: juiced, poached, sautéed and paired with walnuts for salad, and, of course, baked in pastries. My favorite pear varieties for baking include the supple, brown, and easily found Bosc; the rarer and subtler Concorde; and the crunchy-tart Seckel. Pear skin is so thin that I usually leave it intact, but peel your pears if you prefer.

In a large bowl, combine all of the ingredients and mix well. Let stand until the pears give up some of their juices, 20 minutes to 1 hour. Use immediately.

Chocolate-Pear Variation

Years ago on a trip to Paris, I tasted a remarkable pastry in a bakery near the École Militaire. It was a little round of buttery brioche in which a few pear slices and a lick of chocolate were nestled. It was perfection. You can try to make a similar pastry with this filling, some chocolate, and the Flaky Butter Crust (page 108). Add ⅔ cup/115 g bittersweet chocolate chips to the pear mixture before filling the pies. Or, for a more refined pear-chocolate combination, place 1 tsp Bittersweet Ganache Filling (page 134) on each piece of dough before adding the pear mixture. If you decide to forgo portability, serve on a plate with a scoop of salted caramel or burnt sugar ice cream.

Sweet Potato Filling

makes enough for 12 to 16 free-form or structured pies or 6 jar pies

Sweet potato is one of those comforting, stick-to-your-ribs filling flavors that straddle the line between sweet and savory, like pumpkin. Use dark brown sugar if you crave a more pronounced molasses flavor, and ramp up the spices a bit if you want to add bite to your filling. The starchy, bland sweet potato flavor supports aggressive spicing.

1. Preheat the oven to 400°F/200°C/gas 6. Place the sweet potato pieces on a small rimmed baking sheet, and drizzle with the vegetable oil. Bake until tender when pierced with a fork, about 35 minutes. Remove from the oven and let cool completely.

2. In a stand mixer fitted with the paddle attachment, beat the egg until blended. Add the baked sweet potato, brown sugar, milk, butter, vanilla, bourbon (if using), spices, and salt and beat until smooth. (Or, use a large bowl and a handheld mixer or a wooden spoon.)

3. Use immediately, or cover and refrigerate for up to 3 days.

1 large sweet potato, about 1 lb/455 g, peeled and quartered

1 tsp vegetable oil

1 egg

½ cup/100 g firmly packed light or dark brown sugar

¼ cup/60 ml whole milk or buttermilk

2 tbsp unsalted butter, melted

1 tsp vanilla extract

1 to 2 tbsp bourbon or dark rum (optional)

½ tsp ground cinnamon

¼ tsp ground ginger

¼ tsp freshly grated nutmeg

¼ tsp kosher salt

Bittersweet Ganache Filling

makes 1 ½ cups/360 ml, enough for 12 to 16 free-form or structured pies or 6 jar pies

8 oz/225 g bittersweet chocolate, preferably 62 to 72 percent cacao

¾ cup/180 ml heavy cream

2 tbsp unsalted butter, cut into ½-in/12-mm cubes

Ganache, a silky blend of chocolate, butter, and cream, can be used two ways: it makes a great stand-alone filling, such as in Chocolate-Cinnamon Pop Tarts on page 30, and it can be used with other flavors and fillings. For example, you can elevate Pecan Pie (page 55) by stashing a little scoop of ganache on the bottom of the crust. The same goes for a structured pie made with Cherry Filling (page 120). You can substitute 1⅓ cups/225 g bittersweet chocolate chips for the bar chocolate and skip the chopping step.

1. Coarsely chop the chocolate by hand or in a food processor and place in a bowl.

2. In a small saucepan, heat the cream over medium heat just until bubbles form around the edges of the pan. Remove from the heat and pour over the chocolate. Let stand for 5 minutes, then stir with a wooden spoon until smooth. Stir in the butter until melted.

3. Let cool and use immediately, or cover and refrigerate for up to 2 weeks.

Fresh Greens and Cheese Filling

makes enough for 12 to 16 free-form or structured pies or 6 jar pies

This filling has enormous potential for experimentation, and this recipe provides a template for multiple combinations of greens and cheeses. Depending on the cheese and greens you choose to pair, you can vary the flavor profile from Greek to Italian to all-American. Don't go light on the greens or the cheese. The greens cook down to almost nothing, and you want to use enough cheese so that its texture and flavor shine. I prefer the bold flavor of raw onion and garlic (they mellow as the pies bake), but you can sauté them in a little olive oil before you add them to the spinach if you prefer milder pies. Or, you can leave both of them out. I have used spinach and feta here, but you can come up with your own combination. Rachel and I have a number of favorites: escarole and provolone, Belgian endive and Manchego, beet greens and fresh goat cheese, and Swiss chard and Camembert.

1 tbsp olive oil

8 cups/300 g coarsely chopped spinach

1 small yellow onion, minced

1 garlic clove, minced

1½ cups/200 g finely crumbled feta cheese

Salt

Freshly ground pepper

1. In a large sauté pan, warm the olive oil over medium heat. Add the spinach and stir until wilted, about 5 minutes. Remove from the heat, drain in a colander, and let cool completely.

2. Wrap the cooled spinach in a clean kitchen towel and squeeze to press out as much excess moisture as possible. Or, using a large, broad spoon, press against the spinach in the colander to release the excess moisture.

3. In a bowl, combine the spinach, onion, garlic, and cheese and stir to mix well. Season with salt and pepper. Use immediately.

Sources

Amazon.com
www.amazon.com
Excellent source for various hard-to-find ingredients, including crème de menthe, extracts, and malt powder.

Bob's Red Mill
(800) 349-2173
www.bobsredmill.com
High-quality organic flours and cornmeal.

Butterworks Farm
421 Trumpass Road
Westfield, VT 05874
(802) 744-6855
www.butterworksfarm.com
Top-notch granary goods.

Daisy Flour
McGeary Organics
P.O. Box 299
Lancaster, PA 17608
(800) 624-3279
www.daisyflour.com
Small-mill all-purpose and pastry flours: white, whole wheat, and spelt.

Dufour Pastry Kitchens
251 Locust Avenue
New York City, NY 10454
(800) 439-1282
www.dufourpastrykitchens.com
Puff pastry dough.

Flying Pigs Farm
246 Sutherland Road
Shushan, NY 12873
(518) 854-3844
www.flyingpigsfarm.com
Great source for all things pork, including leaf lard and pie crusts.

Full Belly Farm
P.O. Box 251
Guinda, CA 95637
(530) 796-2214
www.fullbellyfarm.com
Small-mill flours.

IGourmet
(877) 446-8763
www.igourmet.com
High-quality fruits and vegetables, pantry items, and baking ingredients.

Prairie Pride Farm
59597 185th Street
Mankato, MN 56001
(866) 245-7675
www.prairiepridepork.com
Leaf lard.

Prather Ranch
P.O. Box 344
Macdoel, CA 96058
www.pratherranch.com
Top-quality leaf lard and pie crusts.

Willamette Valley Fruit Company
2994 Eighty-second Avenue NE
Salem, OR 97305
(503) 362-8678
www.wvfco.com
Top-notch frozen fruits, including cherries, marionberries, apricots, and peaches.

Williams-Sonoma
(877) 812-6235
www.williams-sonoma.com
Pie molds, pastry and baking tools, and ingredients.

Index

A

Abbott, Gregg, 34–35
Apples
  Apple Filling, 128
  Dried Apple and Raisin Filling, 129
Apricot Filling, 127

B

Bacon, Egg, and Cheese Breakfast Pie, 70–71
Banana Cream Pie, 78–79
Beef
  Shepherd's Pie, 95–97
The BitterSweet Bakery, 60–61
Bittersweet Ganache Filling, 134
Blueberry Filling, 126
Busley, Mike and Denise, 122–23
Butter, 14
Buttermilk-Whiskey Pie, 58–59

C

Cheese
  Bacon, Egg, and Cheese Breakfast Pie, 70–71
  Chicken Chile Relleno Pie, 43–45
  Cottage Cheese Pie, 67
  Farmer Cheese Pie, 65–67
  Fresh Greens and Cheese Filling, 137
  Mozzarella, Tomato, and Prosciutto Pie, 39–41
  Orange Marmalade– Mascarpone Pop Tarts, 37–38
  Peanut Butter Pie, 88–89
  Ricotta Cheese Pie, 67
  Shepherd's Pie, 95–97
  Sturdy Cream Cheese Crust, 117–18
Cherry Filling, 120
Chicken
  Chicken Chile Relleno Pie, 43–45
  Chicken Potpie, 98–99
Chile Relleno Pie, Chicken, 43–45
Chocolate
  Bittersweet Ganache Filling, 134
  Chocolate-Cinnamon Pop Tarts, 30–31
  Chocolate Crumb Crust, 106–07
  Chocolate Malt Pie, 87
  Chocolate Mousse Pie, 91
  Chocolate-Pear Filling, 132
  Cocoa Pretzel Crust, 86
  Grasshopper Pie, 92–94
  Vanilla Malt Pie, 86–87
Cocoa Pretzel Crust, 86
Coconut Cream Pie, 80–81
Concord Grape Filling, 119
Confectioners' Sugar Glaze, 33
Cooking tips, 17–18
Corn
  Chicken Chile Relleno Pie, 43–45
  Versatile Cornmeal Crust, 114–15
Cottage Cheese Pie, 67

Crusts
  blind-baked, 18
  Chocolate Crumb Crust, 106–07
  Cocoa Pretzel Crust, 86
  Flaky Butter Crust, 108–09
  flavored, 109
  freezing dough for, 105
  Graham Cracker Crust, 106
  for jar pies, 75, 77
  Luscious Lard Crust, 110–11
  partially baked, 18
  Sturdy Cream Cheese Crust, 117–18
  using prepared dough for, 19
  Versatile Cornmeal Crust, 114–15

D

Double-Crust Jar Pie Master Recipe, 76–77
Dried Apple and Raisin Filling, 129

E

Egg, Bacon, and Cheese Breakfast Pie, 70–71
Elsen, Emily and Melissa, 68–69
Equipment, 12–13

F

Farmer Cheese Pie, 65–67
Fillings
    Apple Filling, 128
    Apricot Filling, 127
    Blueberry Filling, 126
    Cherry Filling, 120
    Chocolate-Pear Filling, 132
    Concord Grape Filling, 119
    *Dried Apple and Raisin
       Filling, 129*
    for free-form pies, 27
    *Fresh Greens and Cheese
       Filling, 137*
    frozen fruit, 105
    Peach Filling, 127
    Pear-Ginger Filling, 132
    Quince Filling, 128
    *Raspberry (or Other Tart
       Berry) Filling, 125*
    *Raspberry-Rhubarb
       Filling, 120*
    Sweet Potato Filling, 133
    tips for, 17
Flaky Butter Crust, 108–09
Flour
    locally milled, 15
    measuring, 16
    types of, 14
Four & Twenty Blackbirds, 65,
    68–69
Free-Form Pie Master Recipe,
    28–29
Freezing
    fruit, 14
    pies, 18
Fresh Greens and Cheese
    Filling, 137
Fruit. See also individual fruits
    choosing, 14
    freezing, 14
    measuring, 16
Frying tips, 20–21
Fulton, Nancy, 112–13

G

Glaze, Confectioners' Sugar, 33
Graham Cracker Crust, 106
Grand Traverse Pie Company,
    122–23
Grapes
    Concord Grape Filling, 119
    *Peanut Butter and Jelly Pop
       Tarts, 32–33*
Grasshopper Pie, 92–94

H

Harvell, Sandra, 22–23
Hoce, Nell, 22–23
Hubig, Simon, 130–31
Hubig's Pies, 130–31

J

Julien Pie Shop, 122

L

Lamb
    Shepherd's Pie, 95–97
Lard, 14
Lasyone, Angela, 100–01
Lasyone's Meat Pie Restaurant,
    100–01
Lemon Meringue Pie, 83–85
Luscious Lard Crust, 110–11

M

Mawmaw's Fried Pies, 22–23
Measuring, 16
Mint
    Grasshopper Pie, 92–94
Mozzarella, Tomato, and
    Prosciutto Pie, 39–41

N

Natchitoches meat pies, 100–01

O

Oh my! Pocket Pies, 43, 46–47
Orange Marmalade–Mascarpone
    Pop Tarts, 37–38
The Original Fried Pie Shop, 112–13

P

Peach Filling, 127
Peanuts
    *Peanut Butter and Jelly
       Pop Tarts, 32–23*
    Peanut Butter Pie, 88–89
Pears
    Chocolate-Pear Filling, 132
    Pear-Ginger Filling, 132
Peas
    Chicken Potpie, 98–99
    Shepherd's Pie, 95–97
Pecan Pie, 55–57
Phillips, Joe, 46–47
Pies. See also individual recipes
    cooking, 17–18
    *Double-Crust Jar Pie Master
       Recipe, 76–77*
    equipment for, 12–13
    *Free-Form Pie Master
       Recipe, 28–29*
    freezing, 18
    frying, 20–21
    ingredients for, 14–15
    rolling out dough for, 16–17
    shaping and filling, 17
    *Structured Pie Master
       Recipe, 53–54*
Pizza dough, 19
Pop tarts
    *Chocolate-Cinnamon Pop
       Tarts, 30–31*
    *Orange Marmalade–
       Mascarpone Pop Tarts,
       37–38*
    *Peanut Butter and Jelly
       Pop Tarts, 32–33*

Potatoes
  Bacon, Egg, and Cheese
    Breakfast Pie, 70–71
  Shepherd's Pie, 95–97
Potpie, Chicken, 98–99
Pretzel Crust, Cocoa, 86
Prosciutto, Mozzarella, and
  Tomato Pie, 39–41
Pumpkin Pie, 63–64

Q

Quince Filling, 128

R

Raisin and Dried Apple
  Filling, 129
Ramsey, Andrew "Drew,"
  130–31
Raspberries
  Raspberry (or Other Tart
    Berry) Filling, 125
  Raspberry-Rhubarb
    Filling, 122
Ricotta Cheese Pie, 67
Russo, Leanna, 60–61

S

Shepherd's Pie, 95–97
Shortening, 15
Smith, Tina Lasyone, 100–01
Smothers, Liz, 122
Spinach
  Fresh Greens and
    Cheese Filling, 137
Structured Pie Master Recipe,
  53–54
Sturdy Cream Cheese Crust,
  117–18

Sugar
  Confectioners' Sugar
    Glaze, 33
  measuring, 16
  types of, 14–15
Sweet Potato Filling, 133

T

Techniques, 16–18
Tomato, Mozzarella, and
  Prosciutto Pie, 39–41
Torok, Joanna, 46–47

V

Vanilla Malt Pie, 86–87
Versatile Cornmeal Crust,
  114–15

W

Whiffies, 34–35

Acknowledgments

Sarah's Acknowledgments

Monumental thanks to my wonderful husband, Joel, who did so many dishes, contributed constructive criticism, exercised extraordinary patience, and was ever ready to taste. It's a good thing you love pie! This project would have died without your support and encouragement, as we worked *waaaay* into the night countless times, up until the birth of our daughter. I could not, would not have finished this book without you. Special thanks as well to Lorena Jones, my fabulous Chronicle colleague, who came up with the idea for this book and trusted Rachel and me to run with it. And to Rachel, I owe you endless gratitude for your mighty talent, giant charm, unending optimism, and wonderful friendship.

Rachel's Acknowledgments

Thanks to my coauthor, Sarah Billingsley, for sharing this project and her penchant for perfect crusts. I am in constant amazement of the hours she spent in the late weeks of her first pregnancy baking, writing, and providing the endless optimism that only a true believer in the power of pint-size pies could deliver. One day I will get to say, I knew you when.

Joint Acknowledgments

Huge thanks to our Chronicle editors, Kate Willsky, who exercised a sense of humor and serious patience during the writing, editing, and production of this book, and Amy Treadwell, who lent her impeccable talents as a sounding board, baker, and taster. Thank you to managing editor Doug Ogan, for contributing organizational vision and for being our most reliable and thoughtful taster. Thanks to everyone who brought the visual elements together in such a tantalizing package: Design Army for the initial vision, Alice Chau for gorgeous design oversight, and Ellen Silverman and team for glorious photography. Deep thanks as well to all the other encouraging Chronicle Books Food & Drink folks who worked hard on this book as they do on every Chronicle cookbook: Claire Fletcher, David Hawk, Tera Killip, Bill LeBlond, Peter Perez, and Ann Spradlin. Hearty thanks to Sharon Silva, our top-notch copy editor, for the careful work, metrics expertise, and the intelligence and humor she brought to this speedy project. We can sleep better knowing this book passed through her hands.

Last but certainly not least, thank you to all of the people and businesses who agreed to be profiled for this book, and especially to those who contributed recipes.